Scuba Diving
With
Disabilities

Scuba Diving With Disabilities

Jill Robinson
A. Dale Fox

Published for
Council for National Cooperation in Aquatics

Published by

Leisure Press
Champaign, Illinois

Developmental Editor: Sue Ingels Mauck
Copy Editor: Laura E. Larson
Production Director: Ernie Noa
Typesetter: Yvonne Winsor
Text Layout: Denise Mueller
Cover Photo: Dave Woodward/Tom Stack and Associates
Photos in Text: Curt Barlow Studios
Illustration on Page 37: Mary Yemma Long
Printed By: Versa Press

ISBN: 0-88011-280-8

Library of Congress Cataloging-in-Publication Data

Robinson, Jill, 1951-
    Scuba diving with disabilities.

    1. Scuba diving. 2. Sports for the handicapped.
I. Fox, A. Dale. II. Title.
GV840.S78R57 1987   797.2'3'088081   86-18532
ISBN 0-88011-280-8

Printed in the United States of America

10 9 8 7 6 5 4 3 2 1

Leisure Press
A division of Human Kinetics Publishers, Inc.
Box 5076, Champaign, IL 61820

Contents

Foreword

Both the medical and diving communities offered considerable resistance to the entrance of disabled persons into the high risk sport of scuba diving. Fortunately, scuba diving proved to be an area where disabled persons intended to be involved, regardless of opposition. Although the number of disabled scuba divers has increased considerably in the past few years, diving clubs for persons with disabilities have existed since the early 1970s.

Most disabilities do not interfere with safe involvement in the sport, but the risks do need to be made clear to all participants. As Jill Robinson points out, however, some of the greatest hurdles to overcome have been society's attitudes about disabled persons. Her chapter "Disability Couth" has application far beyond the sport of scuba diving.

Jill Robinson has spent many hours diving and writing in order to produce a practical, usable manual for those persons seeking information about diving with disabilities. We believe she has done just that. The Council for National Cooperation in Aquatics (CNCA) has sponsored scuba diving research and the development of educational materials in this area for many years. CNCA is pleased today to have been a part of the planning for this manual, which we believe will enable many persons with disabilities to explore and enjoy the underwater world.

Louise Priest
Executive Director, CNCA

Acknowledgments

The authors and the Council for National Cooperation in Aquatics (CNCA) wish to thank the many people who contributed to the completion of this manual. Bob Smith, Chairman of CNCA's Board of Directors, tirelessly provided encouragement, insightful comments, and constructive criticism and facilitated every step of the manual's development. Curt Barlow and his associates, Steve Szabo and Paul Weiss, of Curt Barlow Studios in Washington, DC, generously gave of their time and talents in providing the photographs that illustrate the manual. Bob Tilman of the Diving Site in Marathon, Florida, donated his own time, his boat, Thunderboat, and equipment for a photography session. Pat Walbridge helped with the final photo session, jumping into her suit and gear when another model was needed. John Nelson and Laurie Fernald of Boston's Moray Wheels Adaptive Scuba Association (the Wheels) and Ted Bridis of Miami, Florida, made a special trip to Marathon to model for the photos. Ted also wrote the section discussing his prostheses and designed the drawing that illustrates them. Jack Benedick provided additional information about prostheses used by other amputee divers. Larry Roffee and Mark Sakaley bravely acted as human guinea pigs as we tested and observed some of the techniques described in the manual. John Nelson, Laurie Fernald, and Betsy Pillsbury, members of the Wheels, reviewed the manual and provided helpful comments, as did Lou Nessler, a YMCA instructor in Chicago who has taught many disabled divers. Sharon Mistler, Annette Lauber, and Bob Burgdorf also provided encouragement and comment. Gail Gerebenics and Derryl Stewart King proofread endlessly.

Early in 1983, Charles Shilling, then director of the Undersea Medical Society, convened a meeting of disabled divers, training agency representatives, and other interested parties who identified the development of state-of-the-art information as a priority and began the chain of events that led to the publication of this manual. Carol Beaulieu, the aquatics director of Virginia's Fairfax County Park Authority, also planted seeds that culminated in this project when she took affirmative steps to integrate disabled students (of which the principal author was one) into the county's scuba classes.

Our sincere thanks are extended to everyone who helped make this manual possible.

Introduction

Although people with a variety of disabilities have been diving for years, very little information is available describing how they do it. Consequently, disabled student/dive instructor pairs across the country have had to reinvent the techniques and technologies others already use. The primary purpose of this manual is to make state-of-the art information available for disabled students and divers and their instructors. The creative energies that were used to reinvent the same techniques and technologies will then be available to develop improved methods and advance the state of the art.

Another purpose of the manual, beginning with the next edition, is to let disabled divers, would-be divers, and students know where to find each other and where to find instructors who know how to teach them and to provide a central source of information on the accessibility of various dive shops, boats, and sites. The accomplishment of this purpose depends on reader cooperation in providing the appropriate information about themselves, their colleagues, and the dive shops and sites with which they are familiar. Information submitted by readers will be published in future editions. An appendix contains forms soliciting this information.

At this time, the manual addresses a limited range of disabilities, namely those that result in a weakness in, a complete lack of, or a lack of use of, one or both legs; diminished upper body strength; loss of manual dexterity; and mild respiratory weakness. When students with these disabilities enter the class, the instructor will frequently see a variety of differences from traditional students. Some will use prosthetic limbs that go unnoticed until a pool session. Others will use crutches, canes, or manual or electric wheelchairs. The disabilities result from various conditions such as amputation, paraplegia, or quadriplegia; and they had causes as diverse as car or sport accidents, combat, or illness. Other than the information contained in Appendix A, "Introduction to Selected Disabilities," this manual is not concerned with the sources, general implications, or characteristics of disabilities but rather the effect certain disabilities have on diving. These effects require the use of certain methods, skills, and equipment not always important to divers of average strength.

The manual does not now address the methods used by divers with every type of disability. Thus, although blind people and deaf people, for example, enjoy sport diving, this manual does not now include the ways in which their diving or the methods used to teach them differ from those to which the instructor is accustomed. This omission does not result from a judgment that one disability is more important or more interesting than another but rather simply reflects the authors' lack of expertise. At this stage in our learning about diving with sensory disabilities, we believe that the differences in diving and teaching are clustered mostly around communication techniques. A few other methods, such as those for establishing and maintaining orientation, are necessary. Persons experienced either in diving with disabilities other than the ones addressed in this manual or in teaching diving to persons with these other disabilities are invited and encouraged to contact the authors. We hope to collect enough information and gain enough experience with other disabilities to include information regarding them in the next edition of this manual.

The manual also does not incorporate the considerations applicable when disabled people dive for any reason other than sport diving. While we are aware of a quadriplegic commercial diver (who was recovering bodies from California rivers before buoyancy control devices came into vogue), we do not discuss considerations relevant to the various types of commercial diving. Needless to say, this is not intended as any indication that commercial diving is beyond the abilities of the people whose methods are described in this manual.

Also beyond the scope of this manual are any considerations unique to providing a diving experience for persons whose disability prevents independent sport diving or to diving as a rehabilitative experience. Many seriously disabled people who do not have the abilities necessary to dive independently are able nevertheless to enjoy a guided underwater experience. Very experienced divers can decide for themselves the circumstances under which they may want to provide such experiences. During the rehabilitation of a newly injured person, diving might be an appropriate activity to help the person learn that life is not over, that adventure is still possible, and that a degree of mobility no longer possible on land can be recaptured. In this case, because the newly injured person has not yet learned all the implications of the disability, such as how the body will react to extremes of temperature, the participation of someone familiar with the disability is essential.

Even within sport diving, this manual does not contain guidelines articulating who should and who should not dive or who should and who should not be certified. Any experienced, competent diving instructor should be able to observe a student and evaluate whether or not the student has the potential to become a safe diver. The fact that a student has a disability does not alter an instructor's ability to evaluate basic skills and attitudes.

The experienced instructor is sensitive to the fact that no two students enter a scuba diving class with the same level of basic ability. Indeed, a wide range of physical ability generally exists in classes with no obviously disabled students. The instructor of any diving class is often confronted with students having transient or permanent disabilities such as recent injuries, a delicate lower back, strains and sprains, or students with small frames, weak musculature, poor motor coordination, and so on. The techniques and technologies presented in this manual should be helpful in dealing with these everyday conditions as well as those more commonly considered to be disabilities.

We hope that the publication of this manual will encourage disabled divers and their instructors to come forward with information about additional techniques and technologies they may have developed, as well as their improvements to the ones we suggest. We strongly encourage divers and instructors to send their ideas, inventions, methods, and photos to us for possible inclusion in subsequent editions of this manual. Material should be addressed to Leisure Press, Box 5076, Champaign, IL 61820, marked to the attention of "Dive Manual."

How to Use This Manual

This manual is meant to be a supplement to existing scuba manuals for instructors, students, and divers. It is not a general scuba text and does not contain the basic information all students must learn to dive safely. Rather, it contains only that information not found in other texts about the skills and equipment used by divers who have certain disabilities.

Instructors of students with these disabilities can make good use of the manual by consulting it before teaching a class that covers any of the topics the manual discusses. Students will benefit by reading it in conjunction with the corresponding material in their scuba text and classroom and pool sessions.

The first part, Getting Started, is intended to orient the reader to the manual and to orient instructors and students meeting for the first time to each other.

The second part, Equipment, deals exclusively with the equipment considerations unique to divers with certain disabilities. Instructors and students should read the appropriate section of this part before they select each piece of gear the student will use in the water. If after the first reading the student does not understand what a piece of equipment does or how it functions, this should be of no concern. That information will be provided by the instructor and assigned readings.

Divers who have already been trained and are planning to rent or purchase gear might also benefit from reading the section relating to the item they are considering.

The third part, Skills, discusses those skills that are needed only by divers with certain disabilities (such as achieving proper trim) or that they perform differently (such as ascents and descents). For the skills discussed, only the unique or different techniques are presented. A student cannot learn any basic scuba skill from this manual alone. Only that information not found in other scuba texts is presented. To completely understand the importance and methods of performing all required skills, the student must complete professional scuba training.

The final part of the manual, Matters for the Classroom, discusses a few items that merit a bit more emphasis in the classroom portion of the scuba training. These topics are covered in every basic class, so the instructor need only add a few minutes to the lecture portion of the class and the student should consider the topics a bit more carefully.

Three appendices are included. The first, Introduction to Selected Disabilities, is intended for those instructors who have not known people with these disabilities and are curious about the disability itself. This is not medically precise material, but it will acquaint the instructor with some of the lay terminology often used in the disability community and with some causes and implications of certain disabilities.

The purpose of the second appendix is to gather information on where the disabled community and instructors who have taught disabled divers can find each other and where to find convenient diving. It contains forms that readers are encouraged to use to supply additional information identifying disabled divers and instructors of disabled divers and to evaluate the accessibility of the dive shops, boats, and sites they have visited. Lists of divers and instructors and evaluations of accessibility will be appended to the manual when subsequent editions are published.

The third appendix contains identifying information on the organizations and publications mentioned in the manual. Addresses are not given for the manufacturers or retailers of generally available dive equipment because this equipment is normally purchased from a local dive shop, not from the original supplier.

Getting Started 1

Getting Started 1

Disability Couth

It is a natural human reaction to feel uncertain and apprehensive when faced with any situation outside the realm of past experience. Because disabled people are outside the experience of many nondisabled people, the latter often feel uncomfortable during their first encounter with people with visible disabilities and worry about saying or doing the "wrong thing." Open communication between individuals about their differences and similarities is the best and most effective way for individuals to come to understand and be comfortable with each other. This chapter's purpose is to help alleviate some of the discomfort and anxiety that inhibits open communication by putting disability in perspective, by examining and correcting popular images of disability, and by identifying certain appropriate and inappropriate behavior and language.

This chapter differs in style and is more voluminous than other chapters of the manual. While the rest of the manual presents concise factual information on techniques and technologies used by disabled divers, this chapter is a fairly lengthy examination of more amorphous matters such as feelings and behaviors. It is necessary to learn the techniques and technologies used by disabled divers before you undertake to teach disabled students. However, you don't need to plow through this chapter before doing that. If you get bogged down or don't find it interesting, or if you already have disability couth, move on to the more technical material.

A Disability Is Only That

Every person has an enormous number of physical, mental, emotional, psychological, spiritual, and other characteristics. Everyone possesses each trait in varying amounts, falling somewhere along a spectrum of that characteristic. Where an individual falls on one spectrum (e.g., mental acuity) may be entirely different from where that person falls on another spectrum (e.g., physical strength or emotional stability). No one has the optimum amount of each characteristic, and almost everyone feels the frustration of having less of some valued characteristic than they would prefer. Everyone, then, should be able to understand intuitively that having a physical disability, that is, falling at the low end of the single spectrum of physical strength, does not determine where a person falls on the spectrum of other characteristics.

Unfortunately, this is not so. Our society has identified having a physical disability to be a more significant characteristic than others, and it has created several stereotypes that it portrays as necessarily accompanying a physical disability. Like other stereotypes, they are more often false than true and are a disservice to both the people about whom they are held and the people who hold them. To complicate the matter further, many individuals have very negative associations with some of disability's paraphernalia. It is little wonder, then, that many people combine associations from their own horrifying medical experiences with the pitiful image of disability prevalent in society, resulting in inaccurate and inappropriate stereotypes of people with disabilities. Given a world configured by these stereotypes, it is not odd that many nondisabled people have not interacted with disabled people and often behave inappropriately when they first do.

The next section of this chapter identifies some inaccurate and inappropriate stereotypes commonly held about people with disabilities and offers more factual information as a substitute. The following section provides some tips for appropriate behavior for those who will be encountering people with disabilities for the first time. The final section offers a few words about the prudent use of language.

Common Stereotypes

"Physically disabled people are also intellectually disabled and lacking in good judgment." Divers have been heard to say that disabled people can't dive because they may decide they can do it without a buddy or may dive in currents they can't handle. It should be obvious that any diver may make these bad judgments. A physical disability has no effect whatsoever on mental capacity. Physically disabled people, like nondisabled people, can fall anywhere along the spectrum of mental ability. Divers with disabilities are, therefore, at least as competent as other divers to assess and make decisions about undertaking the risks involved in diving. In fact, some individuals with disabilities may be more accustomed than other people to evaluating a new environment in relation to their abilities.

"People with physical handicaps are generally helpless and dependent; they are used to having people take care of them." Again, the presence of a handicap does not give any indication where along the spectrum of independence a person may fall. Although a disability may influence the amount of independence an individual develops, there is no way to predict what the influence will be. Some people with disabilities may be far more independent than is usual not only by natural inclination but also by having this inclination reinforced from an early age as they were purposefully taught how to function independently during rehabilitation. Other people with disabilities may have been hidden away from the world and protected by oversolicitous parents. The disability of still other people may have had no effect on the degree of their independence. As it is with any other single characteristic anyone may have, the mere presence of a disability gives no indication where along the spectrum of independence an individual may fall.

"Disabled people who need assistance in a specific situation need help with everything and can't carry their weight." People with disabilities often need assistance in particular situations dealing with facilities and equipment designed for others. For example, divers who use wheelchairs often need assistance getting on dive boats because there is usually a significant change of level from the dock to the deck of the boat. Once on the boat, they may need assistance getting a drink of water from the cooler in the cabin, beyond an enormous step. This does not mean that they should be considered helpless for all purposes and discounted when it comes time to do the chores. Some wheelchair users have developed considerable upper body strength. These divers may be even more competent than others at passing tanks down the line as they are off-loaded. Others may have fine-tuned their ability for logistical planning and problem solving and would make excellent divemasters or rescue coordinators.

"People with physical disabilities are sick; their conditions are medical ones." Many people think that people with disabilities are sick, that they belong in a hospital or rehabilitation center, that all their activities should be therapeutic, and that their problems should be dealt with by the medical community. After a disabling illness or injury, people do need medical attention to stabilize their physical condition, to redevelop whatever functional abilities may return, and to learn to compensate for the ones that don't return. Disabilities are the

permanent functional limitations that remain after the medical profession has done its best. Once the rehabilitation process is over, individuals with disabilities interact with the medical community like anyone else—reluctantly and on an as-needed basis. Like other people, they engage in recreational activities for fun, fitness, or a thrill, or to meet people or find a new interest, not for therapy.

Some disabilities do have associated medical problems. For example, quadriplegia and paraplegia often involve a higher incidence of bladder infection. Conversely, some medical problems have associated disabilities. Multiple sclerosis is a disease that brings a variety of disabilities, each of which often changes from time to time. It is nevertheless important to understand the distinction between the disability, that is, the functional limitations that the individual and society must accept and accommodate as a permanent fact, and the transient medical complications or conditions that are sometimes associated and are the only concern of the medical profession.

"People with disabilities are basically different from people without them and are all alike among themselves." Most people know at an intellectual level that this is not true. Nevertheless, behavior often reflects the stereotype. When the elevator doors open to reveal someone sitting in a wheelchair to an otherwise rational person, you might see the latter staring with the wide eyes and dropped mouth normally reserved for aliens from outer space or machine gun-wielding gangsters. You might see an otherwise rational person patting the head of a full-grown adult simply because the latter is sitting in a wheelchair. The server at the restaurant or clerk at the store may totally ignore the disabled person and ask a companion whether he or she, pointing to the disabled person, wants anything else. This behavior reflects an often unconscious conclusion that the person to whom the behavior is directed is so *different* as not really to be a person. Again, falling at an extreme end of the spectrum of one characteristic does not make the whole person completely different from the rest of humanity.

Although everyone knows that blindness or deafness differs significantly from paraplegia, for example, many people do not understand that people with disabilities that look alike may have vastly differing abilities. For example, three students might roll into a scuba class in wheelchairs, looking fairly similar to the uninitiated. However, one student might be a double amputee who will strap on prosthetics and fins and dive in the traditional manner; another might be a paraplegic whose most efficient method of propulsion is a breaststroke; and the third might be a quadriplegic who enjoys using a "dolphin kick" for propulsion. Two divers may look as though they have very similar disabilities, but it may turn out that one has a lot of residual use of leg muscles that provides significant stability in the water whereas the other does not. Even two divers who do, in fact, have very similar disabilities may do things quite differently. One may prefer to sit on the edge of the pool or dock, gear up, and fall in whereas the other may prefer, when possible, to enter the water first and then gear up. People with disabilities are as different from each other as nondisabled people are and have preferences as varied.

"Disabled people are frail and can't do anything rigorous or physically challenging." Some people with disabilities, like nondisabled people, do have medical conditions that make them frail. However, most people with disabilities do not have such medical conditions and are at least as hearty as anyone else. A fair number of people with various disabilities participate in such rigorous activities as skiing, skydiving, marathoning, flying, sailing, hunting, and of course scuba diving.

"Handicapped people are sensitive about their disability and don't want to discuss it." Handicapped people, like fat or bald people or people with any other characteristic devalued by our society, have all achieved a different level of acceptance and ability to deal with their devalued characteristic. Some disabled people are used to their disability and have had the time and ego strength to accept it, become comfortable with it, learn to compensate for it, and develop a healthy self-image that integrates the disability. These people are likely to welcome the opportunity to discuss their disability. By discussing it, both parties acknowledge its existence and can accommodate it in their joint activities.

However, not all disabled people have had the time or ability to peaceably integrate their disability. These people are unlikely to welcome a discussion about it. Rather, they are more likely to deny its existence and hope that others will do the same. They may nevertheless be otherwise well adjusted and successful. When we had an unusually successful president with a disability, the entire nation joined him in denying the fact that he was a wheelchair user. Disabled people vary as much in their ability to be comfortable with their disability as nondisabled people do in their ability to be comfortable with their own devalued characteristics.

Principles for Developing Disability Couth

Eliminate stereotypes about disability from your thinking as well as consequent behaviors. The most important step in acquiring disability couth is to recognize the stereotypes that may cause you to treat people with disabilities inappropriately. To rid your thinking of those stereotypes identified above will take you a long way toward this goal. Intellectual understanding of the inappropriateness of the stereotypes is not enough, however. To loosen their hold you must constantly monitor your behavior for unconscious applications of stereotypical thinking. The process is a lifelong one. Even people who have been disabled for decades must work to make sure that their own thinking and behavior does not simply reflect society's negative assessment of them.

Don't replace one stereotype with another. Some people, when faced with the loss of patterns that helped them understand the world around them, will experience a need to replace them with new patterns. This is why some people who have learned that society's stereotypes about disability are not true invent their own new stereotypes. It is not uncommon for people who are interacting with disabled people for the first time to see patterns that don't exist. It may be that the first three wheelchair users they meet all like music. They may then invent some very good reason to conclude that *all* wheelchair users like music. However, this is no more true than any other stereotype.

Don't participate in the insensitive behavior of others. When you begin to spend time with people with disabilities, you will have the opportunity to observe the manner in which they are sometimes treated by the uninitiated. In fact, the uninitiated may try to draw you into the offending behavior.

Suppose, for example, that you have arrived with your class on the dock and loaded everybody and everything on board. You are standing on the deck talking to one of your students who is sitting in a wheelchair. It's unbearably hot and departure has been delayed. The mate comes up and asks you if the student would prefer to go in the cabin and sit in the shade. The question, of course, is properly addressed to the student, not to you. By addressing it to you, the mate puts you in the role of the student's caretaker and relegates the student to noncompetent-person status. Although it is always difficult to know how to respond in such situations, the important thing is not to answer on the student's behalf. Doing so would affirm the mate's original stereotypical thinking and behavior. If the student does not respond, you might appropriately inform the mate that the student is better suited to answer the question.

Provide assistance only in the manner and to the extent requested. People are often inclined to give assistance when they think it is needed rather than when the person being assisted actually does need it. Unwanted help is very often unwelcome help. Until you develop a pattern with an individual, the appropriate thing to do is to ask whether help is wanted *before* you provide it. If help is not wanted, do not provide it, even though you believe everything would be easier if you did. Until you are so familiar with a particular individual that you know the circumstances in which help is desired, either wait to be asked for help or offer assistance.

Remember that people with disabilities that look similar will not necessarily want the same assistance. One individual may need help getting up a curb, and another may be hindered by untimely assistance if it throws off the delicate balancing and coordination needed to hop a curb. There are often important details about the manner of providing the help that is needed that only the person being helped knows. It is important to learn how best to help. For example, when lifting someone in a wheelchair onto the deck of a boat, almost everyone starts to lift the chair by its arms. On most chairs, the arms will fall out or, more seriously, may fall out in midlift when the small pins that hold them in place break. Be sure you know how to help before you begin.

Help only to the extent requested. A wheelchair user who asks you for a push up a hill may not need or want to be pushed once over the hill. Because your help was needed with one task, don't feel the need to wait to be helpful again. Anyone who has ever been served by a hovering, overanxious waiter knows that the overanxiousness to help can be stifling and intrusive. Disability couth requires that help be provided only in the manner and to the extent requested.

In your role as scuba instructor, your superior knowledge of scuba may make you aware that students need assistance when they are too inexperienced to be aware of their need. It remains appropriate to provide help and guidance in these situations.

Remember to take the needs of your disabled students, colleagues, and friends into account. You are accustomed to accommodating only the needs of nondisabled people, and you do so automatically because your needs are similar. Some effort is needed to remember and take into account the implication of your students', colleagues', or friends' disabilities. For example, during a pool session, you may have your students gear up and then remember something you want to add to your earlier briefing. You call them together again and pass along the information while they stand around with their gear on. Although this is not a problem for walking people, it would be quite an effort for anyone who doesn't stand and walk with gear on. These students would have to remove their gear, get back in their chairs, join the group, listen to the briefing, go back to the edge of the pool, get out of the chairs, and gear up again. Disability couth requires the fore-thought to avoid these problems.

Similarly, it is common on inland dives to have to negotiate a hill to reach the water. Students who don't walk may need assistance bringing their gear and themselves down the hill. They will gear up at water's edge while other students are gearing up at the top of the hill. This is another time when last-minute additions to a briefing are inappropriate. The disabled student, alone at the bottom of the hill, should not lose the benefit of the information being presented. The briefing should not be held until all the students are at the water's edge and everyone can be included.

Another time this principle becomes important is in planning ac-commodations for a dive trip. The accommodations should be acces-sible or adaptable to the most handicapped diver going on the trip. That diver should be consulted as alternative accommodations are evaluated because he or she can best determine whether they will be usable.

A Word on Language

Our use of the language gives us an opportunity both to express and to examine our thoughts. Often our careless or thoughtless use of words reflects unconscious attitudes or assumptions. Many words often used to discuss disability are uncouth because of the image of disability that they reflect and perpetuate. Obviously, this kind of language should be avoided by anyone attempting to demonstrate dis-ability couth.

"Cripple" and "crippled" are words on a par with "nigger." They should *never* be used by people to whom the terms would not be applied.

"Invalid" is as offensive as "cripple." It suggests a complete in-ability to care for oneself and, more importantly, assesses the individual as one who is not a valid person. It is taboo under all circumstances.

"*The* disabled," "*the* handicapped," or worse, simply "disabled" or "handicapped," when used to refer to people who have a disability or a handicap, reflect and perpetuate a depersonification of those people. These terms take the person out of the concept and substitute the disability as the only significant factor. The fact that a whole person exists with thousands of other characteristics is made irrelevant by the use of such phrases. "People with disabilities" or "individuals with handicaps" puts the concepts "person" and "disability" in their proper perspective.

Other words tend to describe various disabilities inaccurately and offensively. No one is "confined" to a wheelchair. The imagery is of an intolerably horrid life sentence from which there is no escape. The fact is that a wheelchair is a liberating device that enables people who otherwise could not do so to move from place to place. No handcuffs permanently attach the user to the chair, and although many uses of wheelchairs are possible, people do not generally sleep, swim, ski, or make whoopee in them. They are tools to be used or left behind, as needed. "Wheelchair user" and "person who uses a wheelchair" are appropriate phrases. "Victim of polio" (or of a car accident or of a hand grenade) suggests a helpless person who can do nothing to better the situation. The term seems to be a commentary on the fact that the person has limitations. The passive, helpless image it conveys is inappropriate for most survivors, who have worked hard to regain maximum function and who actively fight a constant battle to live in a world designed without regard for their existence. More appropriate phrases would refer to a person "who had polio" or "was in a car accident."

Of some chagrin to those aspiring to disability couth are the situations in which disabled people disagree firmly and sharply over the usage of particular terms. The argument over the relative merits of "disabled" and "handicapped," when used in conjunction with "person" (as "disabled person" or "handicapped person"), is a prime example of this problem. Although the words are commonly used to denote the same thing, that is, unspecified functional limitations, many people with disabilities have a strong distaste for one and a preference for the other. Disability couth requires that those preferences be respected by anyone not themselves affected by the controversy.

Any society forms and is formed by the language it uses. The language our society has used to discuss people with disabilities and the activities in which they engage has reflected and perpetuated the stigmatization of people with disabilities. It is entirely appropriate, then, that these individuals have sensitivities about the language the rest of society uses to discuss them. Disability couth requires that these language sensitivities be accepted and respected. More importantly, disability couth requires the recognition, in word and deed, that people with disabilities are a normal and healthy part of society.

Selecting an Instructor and Club

Many scuba instructors have little or no experience teaching disabled students to dive. This need not be a big concern. You will need to experiment with various techniques and gadgets to find what works best for you. Any well-qualified, experienced, and willing instructor should be able to teach you to dive using the hints in this manual and your own creativity. When you choose an instructor, make sure that he or she is affiliated with a reputable dive shop, YMCA, or college or university and offers certification from one of the nationally recognized certifying agencies (e.g., NASDS, NAUI, PADI, SSI, YMCA). Instructors are trained by one of these certifying agencies, and in order to maintain their authority to certify students, instructors must use that agency's standards.

Some agencies and individual instructors are more receptive to the idea of training disabled divers than others. Most agencies' standards, developed with nondisabled divers in mind, contain requirements that are inappropriate for disabled divers. One agency has had a long-standing policy encouraging their instructors to certify any diver who can master the necessary skills, regardless of the exact wording of their certification standards. Another agency, on the other hand, is still reluctant to certify divers who do not meet the literal requirements of each of its certification criteria. Thus, agencies like the latter would not accept a substitution of a requirement that the student demonstrate proficiency in surface and underwater propulsion for its usual requirement that the student demonstrate proficiency at swimming on the surface and underwater with fins using the flutter kick. Agencies like the former would accept this substitution, on the grounds that it is propulsion, and not the method of propulsion, that is important for safe diving.

When you are interviewing instructors, therefore, you will want to check which organization's certification they offer and determine whether the instructor will be able to certify you if you master the necessary skills. Although any training experience that meets a national agency's criteria will improve your ability to safely explore the underwater world, not all training leads to certification. Without certification, you cannot rent gear, dive off a charter boat, or get your tanks filled with air.

Apart from the possibility of achieving certification, you should consider how a potential instructor's attitude toward people with disabilities will affect the quality of the training provided. Some instructors may begrudgingly accept you for training although they don't believe you should dive. Although this kind of instructor may challenge you more than other students, perhaps providing you with more rigorous training, you may find it distracting to be constantly proving yourself when you should be focusing your attention on learning.

At the other extreme are instructors who enthusiastically solicit many handicapped students for their first experience teaching disabled students and those who are motivated by a need to "help the handicapped." The first type of instructor, all of whose personal experience and training are limited to the techniques and technologies used by nondisabled divers, does not have the knowledge or experience to provide quality training to a number of disabled students simultaneously. This instructor must learn, during the teaching process, about the effects of various disabilities and the skills and methods used by divers with those disabilities. This knowledge simply cannot be gained in one five-week course, with the instructor's attention divided among students with several unfamiliar disabilities. Avoid classes with many disabled students if they will be taught by instructors inexperienced with the skills and methods used by disabled divers.

Instructors motivated by a need to help the handicapped also may not provide quality instruction. Any help you may need in the course, like the help needed by all students, should be incidental to the training you receive, not vice versa. Viewing students as needy and helpless lowers expectations for performance and reduces the quality of training. To become a safe and responsible diver, you need top-notch training. It is especially important when selecting a dive instructor to choose one whose performance will not be marred by paternalistic or condescending attitudes.

Once you've completed basic training, it is a good idea to join a dive club. You can safely reinforce and expand your skills by diving with more experienced club members. Most communities have one or more dive clubs that can be located through local dive shops. Dive clubs that emphasize diving with disabilities are springing up all over the country. Their classes are specially designed to include a number of disabled students, and graduates often become club members and continue to dive with the club.

The usual advantages and disadvantages of a mainstream versus a specially designed program apply, with a couple of additional considerations. Scuba is a sport in which you are likely to need help if inaccessible environments slow you down. Not only will you need to get yourself down the steep, muddy hill to the quarry, but you will also need to get your gear there. If you use a wheelchair, this will often mean that you need one or two people helping you reach the water with your gear. If you dive with a regular class or dive club, you can spread this work without imposing too heavily on anyone. On the other hand, if you dive with lots of people who also need help, the work gets spread over a smaller number of people. You will also want to consider space when diving off a dive boat. A wheelchair takes up a lot of room on a dive boat; several wheelchairs take up even more room. Whereas a walking person with the skills of a mountain goat can move around under these conditions, you won't be going anywhere easily.

The main advantage of a special program is that others have gone before you to lessen the resistance of the uninitiated to a disabled person participating in what many think of as a macho sport. It is an unfortunate truth that many people in the diving industry still assume that disabled people cannot dive safely regardless of their certification or demonstrated level of proficiency. Coming face-to-face with people with such beliefs can be an unpleasant and debilitating experience. Breaking through these barriers on your own is bearable once in a while but not every time you want to dive.

You can also avoid the necessity of constantly breaking through these barriers yourself by joining a reputable dive club with an active dive schedule. Clubs that offer a dive or dive trip every weekend of the season have most frequently been diving with a variety of shops or boat captains for many years. Once you break into the club and are accepted by its members, you won't have to sell yourself to the shops or captains with which they dive. They will assume the club wouldn't bring you along if you weren't qualified to dive.

If you continue diving, you will still have to prove yourself, but you can minimize the unpleasantness by selecting a good instructor and a good dive club.

Notes for Instructors on Access

Access is always a consideration when a dive site is evaluated. Can you get there without rappeling down (or more importantly, climbing back up) a cliff? When you have students who use wheelchairs or other mobility aids, you will want to give this factor more consideration. The first important principle in assessing access is to do it *with* the student. If you don't, you may eliminate a site that has steps down to a dock only to find out that your wheelchair user can negotiate steps in some circumstances or can handle them with some assistance.

Once you begin going places with your students, you will naturally and easily learn about access and the surprising lack of it. But before then, you may wonder how to select a pool that will be comfortable for a wheelchair user. Generally, most people who use wheelchairs do not negotiate steps or other abrupt changes in grade, including extremely steep ramps. Carrying tanks and other dive gear makes handling these barriers even more difficult. People using wheelchairs also do not fit through narrow doors and require more turning space than do individuals standing up. Because people who use wheelchairs are at sitting height, gadgets like mirrors, towel dispensers, drinking fountains, and telephones cannot be reached if they are hung too high on the wall. All of this does not mean that your wheelchair student can only use buildings specially designed to accommodate handicapped people. If the building is adequately ramped or at ground level with none of the barriers described in any of the areas you will be using, it may be usable by your student. If you think there may be a problem with your facility, have a prospective student tour it before signing up for the class.

Most open-water sites are not very accessible. The more accessible ones can be approached closely by car; have terrain that is flat, hard, and level to the water; and drop off immediately at water's edge. Because such sites are rare, disabled divers often must dive at inaccessible sites and deal with the barriers with a buddy's help.

Boat diving is often easier. Access considerations for boats include how it is approached and boarded from the dock (and again, how close you can park the car); how much room there is once aboard for maneuvering; whether the head and other areas are on the same level (this is unusual); what is available to hold onto or wedge into to help stabilize the chair in rough seas; the location of the area from which the water is entered; whether there is a dive platform (this helps a lot); the height of the transom (the lower the better); and the ladder used to get back into the boat. Once again, a convenient combination is rare, and disabled divers frequently must make do and get a little help with the barriers.

Access considerations don't stop at the pool, classroom, and dive site. Don't forget to check the access at the beer joint where the group gathers after class (including the restrooms). If you will be taking the students out of town for checkouts, remember that everywhere you go will need to be accessible. That includes stops along the highway, restaurants, dive shops, lodging, and all the amenities such as showers. More accessible options are available among these facilities. Your disabled students and dive buddies will appreciate the independent mobility that access here allows, especially after encountering a restrictive predive environment.

Preclass Preparation

As you read through this manual, you will notice that there are some factors that are crucial to divers who do it all with their arms but that are of little importance to other divers (the selection of a buoyancy control device [BCD] and other gear, for example). You will also notice that these students must learn skills that are more complex than the comparable task when accomplished by students who use legs for balance and propulsion (maintaining orientation in the water, for example). These students' pool time, therefore, is even more valuable than that of other students. To make the best use of pool sessions, instructors teaching disabled students for the first time should become thoroughly familiar with the skills and methods presented in this manual before the sessions begin. Instructors can also save a lot of pool time by taking time before class to select and fit the proper gear for the student to use in class (see "Equipment"). Instructors should ensure the availability of (a) a properly fitting jacket BCD with all the features described in "Buoyancy Control Devices;" (b) weights that can be placed and balanced properly on the weight belt; and (c) weights and buoyancy devices that can be moved around easily to facilitate experimenting with trim.

Some disabled students, like those with limited manual dexterity, will need assistance with some tasks, such as hauling and assembling gear and entering and exiting the pool. The instructor and the student will both be more comfortable and function more smoothly in class if they each understand before class what help will be needed and how it will be provided. Remember that students won't know what help they need until they know what tasks they must accomplish.

Some disabled students need more time to change into and out of their bathing suits. These students should be encouraged to put on their suits before they come to class to minimize the loss of pool time. To make sure their students have left locker rooms by the facility's closing time, instructors should take extra time requirements into account.

During a preclass discussion, students who lack sensation in their legs and feet should be warned that during pool sessions, their legs and feet are likely to drag or bump against the rough walls and bottom of the pool. They can protect their skin by wearing pants and socks. These students should also be warned that during the gearing-up process, they will be sitting on the hard deck, wiggling into their gear. Students prone to skin breakdown can take necessary precautions (such as sitting on a pad or cushion).

Instructor preparation, the selection of proper gear, and open instructor-student communication before class can make the class a more enjoyable and more valuable training experience and maximize the use of the limited training time available. The importance of this preclass preparation cannot be overemphasized.

Equipment 2

Equipment   2

Buoyancy Control Devices

The selection of a buoyancy control device (BCD) becomes increasingly important with decreasing ability to use the trunk and legs for balance, stability, and vertical movement. In addition to helping the diver control buoyancy underwater, the BCD provides support on the surface. Selection of the right BCD is very important for both functions.

Considerable effort is expended using the arms alone to hold the body vertical in the water at the surface, especially when other factors such as a wet suit or a horse collar are pushing the diver over on the back. Because both arms are usually needed to do so, other tasks, such as manipulating the inflate/deflate mechanism, cannot be accomplished simultaneously. People whose legs lack the strength to hold them vertical while at the water's surface therefore rely on the BCD to do so. Consequently, the proper BCD is essential and should be selected before the first water session.

Jacket for Stability

Only a jacket-type BCD facilitates proper body orientation at the surface. The jacket BCD adds air both in front and in back (and sometimes under the arms) and generally will hold its wearer in a vertical or head-high position on the surface. The horse collar-type BCD, on the other hand, with all its air in front and behind the neck, is designed to roll unconscious divers on their backs at the surface. The horse collar will also push divers without strong legs over onto their backs and hold them there unless they use a lot of upper body energy to overcome its effect. Even in mild seas, this position increases the possibility of aspirating water as waves knock about the mask and regulator and splash water over the face. In this position, it is also difficult for the diver to see what is happening in the immediate area. BCDs that add all the air behind the diver create the opposite problem, with the more serious implication of holding the diver face down in the water. A jacket

A horse collar–type BCD pushes a diver over on her back.

A jacket-type BCD holds a diver vertical on the surface.

BCD should be used from the first water session by any student lacking the lower body strength to maintain a vertical position at the surface.

Soft-Touch Power Inflator, Dump Cord

Most divers now prefer to use a power inflator fed by the scuba tank. Divers with less than optimal lung power definitely benefit from the use of a power inflator, which saves the effort of orally inflating the BCD. Students who will be using their arms for propulsion and stability in the water will also benefit from the use of a power inflator. Any diver should be able to begin inflating the BCD instantly and while doing other things, such as shifting body position or pushing into an ascent. The most efficient way to inflate a BCD manually requires two hands, one for the regulator and one for the inflator hose. Divers who use their hands for movement in the water will not be able to control their body position in the water for very long with both hands occupied like this. The use of a power inflator frees one hand for stability and other tasks.

Inflate buttons differ greatly in the amount of pressure required to operate them. Divers with limited manual dexterity and upper body strength typically use their right palm or the ball of the hand to push the inflate button, which is wedged against the left palm. A soft-touch, or very easily operated power inflator, is crucial in these circumstances. It is a good idea to hook the inflator up to a tank in the store and make sure it can be operated easily before choosing a BCD with a power inflator.

Divers with limited manual dexterity also benefit from the quick-dump valves that are operated by pulling down on a hose or cord and rolling to position the dump valve high. This saves not only the time and effort required to locate and manipulate the dump button but also makes it unnecessary to hold the hose high.

Inflate/Deflate Modification

The inflate/deflate procedure used by divers with limited manual dexterity, namely wedging the hose against the left palm and depressing the button with the right palm, can be time-consuming and inconvenient. Minor modifications to the BCD may permit easier and quicker use of the inflate/deflate mechanism. One idea, which we have yet to build and test, expands on the same principle used in the quick-dump mechanisms in existing BCDs. The dump valve at the top of the

A diver deflates his BCD by pressing the deflate button between his palms.

large inflation hose is connected to the oral power inflator by a thin wire. When the diver pulls down sharply on the inflation hose, the wire opens the quick-dump valve. A modification that puts a large flange around the oral inflator would create an easy target for divers with limited manual dexterity. It could be caught and activated by the V of the hand, between the thumb and index finger. The strength of the shoulder, rather than the fingers, would be used to deflate the BCD by pulling down on the hose.

A similar modification could make inflation as quick and easy as this method of deflation. The BCD would be equipped with an inflation/deflation hose on each side of the BCD. On one side would be the deflation hose, attached to a quick-dump as described in the previous paragraph. The other hose would be connected to the power inflator that would be rigged to activate by pulling down on the hose, not by pressing a button. This hose would also be rigged with a flange to enable it to be lodged between the V of the hand so that the inflator would be activated using the strength of the shoulder rather than the fingers.

Two Pockets

Every diver sometimes finds it more convenient to place a couple weights in a BCD pocket than to add weight to a weight belt. This procedure might save time and effort for divers experimenting to determine how much weight they need; divers who have jumped in the water and found themselves to be too buoyant; divers wearing a little more rubber than they usually do; divers switching from a 72-cubic-foot steel tank to an 80-cubic-foot aluminum tank; and divers carrying positively buoyant objects. Divers who rely partly on weights to maintain good body orientation will need to distribute weight added to BCD pockets evenly on both sides. With many BCDs, this would be impossible because they only have one pocket on one side. BCDs with a pocket on each side are available and should be selected by divers to whom balance is important.

Because ditching a diver's weight is sometimes necessary to facilitate a rescue, adding weight anywhere other than the weight belt is generally discouraged. Wearing weight in a pocket should never become a standard or frequent practice. On those rare occasions when it is appropriate, only a small portion of the total weight a diver wears should be added to a BCD pocket.

Straps and Fit

Shoulder and crotch straps can mean a better fitting BCD that stays in place on the diver and thus provides more stability for the diver. However, straps also make the gearing-up process more difficult. Shoulder straps catch the arm as it is inserted into the armhole of the BCD. Crotch straps are difficult to position while sitting and remove the option of putting the weight belt on before the tank. For these reasons, it is desirable to eliminate the need to use straps. BCDs come in small, medium, and large sizes. It is important to select the proper size from the outset. First-time jacket users often will be convinced that they need the crotch strap to keep the BCD from strangling them when actually the BCD was two sizes too large and the sides were not adjusted tightly. Proper adjustment of a properly sized BCD often eliminates the need for crotch straps.

Some of the better BCDs have eliminated the use of straps by other features assuring a good fit. Several models have removed shoulder straps altogether. Other models come equipped with shoulder straps

After this BCD was rethreaded to eliminate shoulder straps, the backpack was bolted in place.

that can be rethreaded so the straps do not go around the shoulders. Because the original threading in these models stabilizes the backpack in the BCD, it is necessary to bolt the backpack to the BCD when it is rethreaded so the tank will not flop around.

Location of Buoyancy

Several manufacturers now offer a jacket BCD that has only straps over the shoulders and upper chest, instead of the traditional design in which that area inflated when air was added. The new design has two significant advantages: (a) Many divers at depth tend to be naturally light in the upper body, and removing buoyancy from that area facilitates achieving good trim; and (b) divers who use a breaststroke for propulsion have less friction of the upper, inner arm against the BCD when only a strap lies over the upper chest.

Fitting the BCD in Class

A jacket BCD should be available from the first water session. You will want to fit the BCD without the tank first. Frequently, an instructor will simply bring all of the gear available for training to the first pool session. After each student has picked up one of everything, the instructor talks the class through putting it all together. When using jacket-type BCDs, this often results in having the tank already attached to the jacket by the time the jacket is adjusted for fit. To adjust it at this point, the student must sit on the deck in front of the tank. This is the most difficult way to fit it. When students need to lift a buttock to position the crotch strap, for example, they need not only to balance themselves but the tank as well. This can become a labor- and time-intensive exercise.

Achieving the proper jacket fit is crucial. If the jacket rises high in the water, leaving the student behind with mouth underwater, it has not served its purpose and has created quite a problem for a student who is unable to kick. If crotch straps are needed, they should be pulled as tight as possible without damaging the diver's anatomy. Students who have no feeling in this area will want to be especially careful at this stage of the fitting process. Students who use external plumbing that they leave in place in the water will also want to be sure a blockage does not occur.

Proper fit around the waist is also important. A loose jacket will mean a tank flopping around on the diver's back, drastically altering weight distribution and making side-to-side orientation in the water difficult to maintain. Most jackets can be adjusted at the sides as well as the front. If one side is adjusted to be a little looser than the other, it will be easier to put on and remove the jacket by putting on the looser side last and taking off that side first.

Proper BCD Is Critical

A BCD is the single most important piece of gear for divers who use their arms for balance, stability, orientation, and propulsion. Until the BCD is right, the student will be uncomfortable and will either be unable to maintain proper positioning or will have to work excessively to do so. Attention to other tasks will be compromised if the student is spending mental and physical energy just staying in position.

Finding the right BCD and fitting it properly should be accomplished before attempting any other tasks. If modifications to the BCD would be an advantage, the student might benefit from purchasing a BCD before water training begins.

Weight Belts

The selection of weights and a weight belt is important for students who will use their arms for orientation and balance in the water, who have no feeling around the waist, or who have limited manual dexterity. Divers who use their arms for orientation and balance place their weights carefully near center front to counterbalance the weight of the tank and help avoid side-to-side roll (see "Trim"). Hip weights, which are curved to fit the side of the body, may be uncomfortable worn in the front. Bullet weights cannot be doubled up the way square blocks can, and they stretch around the belt if a lot of weight is needed. Depending on their size, one, two, or more square block weights can be threaded simultaneously through the weight belt, creating many more options for their location.

Because the placement of weights is so important, they must be held in place on the belt. This is done by using either weight-belt clips or a longer weight belt that has enough length to be twisted between the slots in the weights.

Many students, especially those who don their gear sitting down, sometimes let the weight belt fall down onto the hips while donning it rather than fastening it at the waist. When the student goes down and becomes prone in the water, the belt slides back up to the waist, loosens, and begins to slide around. The shifting weight pulls the student with it. Students who have no feeling at the waist and hips are not naturally reminded that it is the weights that are causing the problem. Every effort should therefore be made to fasten the weight belt snugly at the smallest part of the waist when it is first donned.

If it is difficult for a student to do this consistently, the student might prefer one of the stretchable types of weight belts, such as the neoprene weight belt. If these belts are stretched a bit and tightly fastened before the dive, they will stay in place even on the hips. Stretchable weight belts are also good for students with limited manual dexterity who don't want to bother opening and closing the buckle when their wet suits compress during descent, thereby loosening the belt.

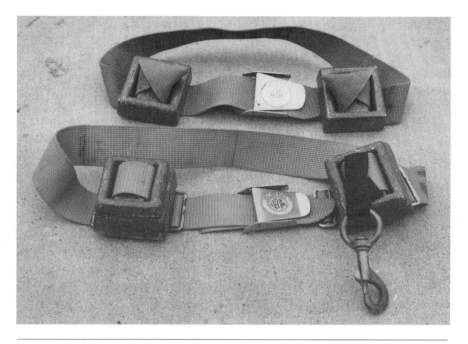

The weights on the weight belt on top are held in place by twists in the weight belt. Two square block weights are stacked on each side of the weight belt on the bottom to keep the weight centralized and are held in place by weight-belt clips or keepers.

Another self-adjusting alternative would be the soft fabric, lead-shot weight belts. Without the hard angles of block weights, these weight belts can be more comfortable than the traditional ones. Because it is difficult and time-consuming to change the amount of weight on these belts, the diver might want to consider adding clip-on block weights when they need more weight.

Students with reduced respiratory power may find it more difficult to breathe wearing a tightly fastened weight belt or BCD strap. If, for example, a student has tightened a belt (or strap) over a compressed suit at depth and has returned to the surface but can't catch his or her breath, an overly tight weight belt (or strap) may be the problem.

Instead of passing a heavy weight belt up to someone on a boat with no dive platform and a high transom, divers who will remove their gear in the water may want to rig a system to hold the weight belt until it can conveniently be pulled up. An effective system is one like that often used by photographers to hold their equipment when entering and exiting the water. If a snap hook has been looped on the weight belt, it can be snapped onto an O ring on the end of a line attached somewhere at the stern of the boat near the ladder. Snapping the weight belt on a line ensures that it won't be lost or fall on someone below if it slips out of the diver's or receiver's hand. When the weight belt is removed, it should be held clear of the diver before it is released. The line should be slack enough that rough seas won't jerk the diver around while the belt is snapped to the line.

Masks

The most important consideration in selecting a mask is always good fit. A poorly fitted mask will leak, necessitating frequent clearing. Because clearing a mask requires the use of one hand, this can be a bother when both hands are needed for other tasks such as swimming and maintaining orientation.

Different masks hold diverse amounts of water when flooded. Low-volume masks hold a relatively small amount of water and therefore

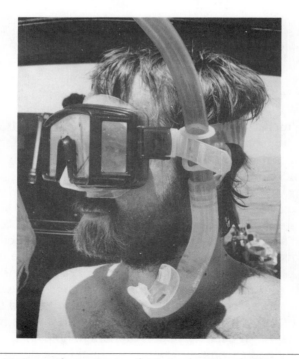

A low-volume, tri-view mask permits easy clearing and peripheral vision.

require less air to clear. A low-volume mask is an asset to all divers but is especially convenient for divers with reduced lung power and divers who want to use less time clearing their mask.

Some masks are equipped with a purge valve that enables mask clearing without using the hands. Most divers find mask clearing such a quick and simple task that the one-way purge valve in these masks is of little value. However, students who cannot master mask clearing in the traditional manner may benefit from the use of a low-volume mask with a purge valve.

Masks also vary widely in the amount of vision they allow a diver. Some are constructed so that the diver's peripheral vision is quite limited. Other masks allow the diver a great deal of peripheral vision. Divers who swim with their arms will find that their buddies tend to swim far off to their side or behind their arm stroke to avoid contact. To enable them to keep track of their buddies, these divers will want to use a mask providing maximum peripheral vision.

Some masks allow divers a good view down the front of their bodies. Some divers find it easier to fasten all the buckles and gadgets that attach in this area if they can look down at them.

A "shotgun"-type snorkle is virtually self-clearing.

Snorkles

Students with limited lung power or a limited range of motion in the neck find self-draining snorkles easier to clear than traditional ones. These snorkles have a purge valve at their lowest point that allows them to drain to water level. Only a little water remains in the snorkle for the diver to blow out.

Snorkles with a flexible, corrugated hose allow faster and easier placement of the mouthpiece into the mouth and should be considered by students whose hands will always be busy. The inside of the corrugated portion of the hose may have a smooth bore or a corrugated bore. The smooth bore snorkle costs a little more, but it is easier to clear than the one with a corrugated bore.

Students who may continue their diver education through rescue training may want to consider that a snorkle with a purge valve cannot easily be used in mouth-to-snorkle resuscitation, whereas a snorkle with a flexible hose is much easier to use for that rescue technique.

Webbed Gloves

People who use their arms for propulsion and who have strong fingers can add considerable strength to their stroke by wearing webbed gloves. These gloves have material filling in the otherwise empty spaces between the spread fingers. By spreading and curving the fingers while stroking, a cup is formed in the hand, greatly increasing its pull in the water. For such a seemingly minor change, these gloves make an enormous difference. They are particularly useful in currents and are a good item to have stored in a BCD pocket.

Webbed gloves are somewhat difficult to find but are available by mail order from Eddie Bauer and from The Finals (see Appendix C for ordering information). The Eddie Bauer glove is of a stronger, more rigid material that has little bumps all over the palm side to facilitate picking up or grasping objects. The Finals' glove is softer and more supple with the ends of the three middle fingers cut out. Because it is easier to feel objects through The Finals' glove, it may be more suitable if the diver will be working with lines. The Eddie Bauer glove, on the other hand, adds more power to the stroke.

Webbed gloves add a lot of power to this diver's stroke.

Fins

Fins on Feet

Some students with weak leg muscles may be able to develop a productive kick by using carefully chosen fins.

Different fin styles vary in the rigidity of their blades. Very rigid fins provide more thrust through the water but require greater leg strength to use. Fins that are too flexible will be easy to move through the water but will provide little thrust. Divers with weak legs may acquire a more useful kick with more flexible fins.

Some fins have solid blades and others have vented blades. Vented fins reduce water resistance when changing the direction of fin movement. For this reason, they may benefit divers with leg muscles barely strong enough to produce any kick.

Weight is another consideration fr ⁻ divers with weak legs when selecting fins. The newer silicone or graphite fins are much lighter than the old rubber fins. In fact, the difference in ease of use between the heavy rubber fin and the lightweight silicone and graphite fin may outweigh the difference between a solid blade fin and a vented blade fin.

There is a new fin on the market, called a "Force Fin," that the manufacturer claims provides more propulsion with less effort than any of the traditional fins. Made of lightweight polyurethane, the fin reportedly folds down on the upkick to reduce water resistance and then snaps open for full power on the downstroke. The manufacturer's claim has been disputed by at least one dive authority, so it is wise to test the fin before purchasing it.

Divers who have muscle weakness only in the ankles or only in the ankles and lower leg might want to look for or replicate a fin that Faralon once made. The fin was attached to a brace that fastened on the calf. On the upstroke of the fin, the blade was free to flex. On the downstroke, the brace held the blade in position and transferred the work of the stroke up to the calf muscles. The fin could easily be modified by elongating the brace so the muscle work was done higher up on the thigh.

Fins on Prosthetics

Some single and double leg amputees find they can get a powerful kick by attaching fins to waterproof prostheses. Because the technology has not become standard, diving prostheses and the methods to attach fins vary widely. One double above-the-knee amputee diver, Ted Bridis of Miami, Florida, describes his prostheses and his experience with their development:

> I got my swimming prostheses in 1972 from J.E. Hangar, which is a national chain of prosthetic shops. My prosthetist was not experienced with swimming prostheses, although he was a single below-the-knee amputee and scuba diver. We invented my prostheses using common sense and available shop technology. I have since found we were reinventing the wheel. This was impressed upon me in a rerun of a "You Asked For It" television show from 1954. It showed a man using the same design but with carved wooden sockets and metal fins. He used them to walk, swim, dive from a spring board, scuba dive and, with the aid of springs on the bottom, to run and play tennis. Most of the amputees I have talked to have also invented their own prostheses. The most unusual was a single below-the-knee amputee who split a fin and glued it to either side of the calf of his prosthesis. He claimed the advantage of being able to swim or walk without changing extremities. The best pool of information probably exists through the National Handicapped Sports and Recreation Association, the snow skiers from Colorado.

My swimming prostheses are constructed as follows: The upper part that fits the stump, called the socket, is single-walled fiberglass, as opposed to a double-walled socket that has a smaller socket fitted exactly to the stump and suspended inside an outer shell. The single-walled socket is open on the inside all the way to the bottom of the socket. It is supported mostly by skin friction on the side walls, although there is an ischial seat. (An ischial seat is a small flange along the back rim of the socket upon which the ischium is supported. The ischium is one of three bones that make up the hip and the one that protrudes through the lower buttocks. Most above-the-knee prostheses transmit body weight to the prosthesis by an ischial seat.) The interior flanges on my first swimming legs acted like scissors on my groin. I remember a particularly terrifying water flume ride that worked my legs open and closed at each turn. On my next set, the flanges were well tapered so that flesh did not overhang. I have come to realize that there is no need for pain during the fitting of sockets. If they hurt in the clinic they will cut or rub sores in the real world.

My sockets were made equal in length so that I could stand up straight. Rubber pads were glued to the bottom to provide a nonslip walking surface. Holes were drilled in the sides at the bottom so water could flow in and out. Each socket is held on with a Sicilian belt, a strap from the front of the socket over the opposite hip around the back to the front of the socket again. The strap is nylon webbing padded with cotton and held with a small buckle. Because my right leg ampu-

The fin fits on the prosthetic foot. The metal bar attached to the foot inserts into a slot on the prosthetic leg.

The prosthetic leg is designed to facilitate standing and walking while still on the boat or land.

tation was a knee disarticulation and my knee cap was left, it fits into a groove in the front of the socket almost like a key. This holds my right socket on very securely and the strap acts only as a backup.

The feet are removable wooden prosthetic feet aligned parallel to my body. A metal rod is screwed to the top of the ankle extending to its rear. The screws and the end attached to the ankle are encased by the fiberglass finish. The rod thus protrudes about 18 inches to the rear of the ankle towards and parallel to the socket. A piece of formed metal about 8 inches long with a hat-shaped cross section is riveted to the front of the socket. This forms an enclosed groove into which the rod of the foot slides. In the first design, thumb screws were mounted on the metal piece to hold the rod in place. Two problems arose. The thumb screws were subject to severe saltwater corrosion and the rods were easily bent with a strong kick. Both problems were solved by eliminating the thumb screws and installing a Velcro strap from the bottom of the foot to the back of the socket. The strap is screwed to the bottom of the foot and runs through a ring that is riveted to the socket. The advantages of this design are: It uses a normal-shaped foot, to which any fin can be fitted, the feet and fins are easily removed for walking around a boat, and the sockets offer good stump protection for other sports such as whitewater rafting.

My stumps change size from time to time. One reason is overall body weight, another is fitness. During the summer when I swim a lot my overall body weight might go down, but my legs increase in bulk as

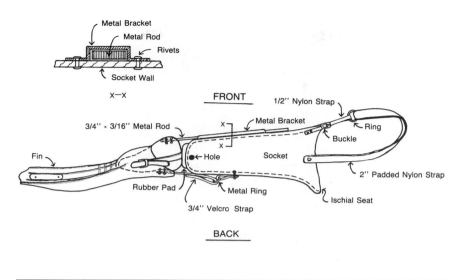

Ted's prosthesis.

my atrophied muscles develop. Sometimes they just swell up with fluid. This can be alleviated if necessary by wrapping with elastic bandages overnight. They also shrink from water pressure. On my early dives over 60 feet, I had problems with my legs being too loose in the sockets, so loose that one time a leg actually fell off. I now pay particular attention to my straps on deeper dives. I wear stump socks to eliminate friction in putting the sockets on. When I am overweight this is very necessary in order to squeeze in and at that time the socks must be dry and powdered.

Ted also notes that buoyancy is a consideration when crafting prostheses for diving. If they are either too positively or too negatively buoyant, the energy that should be used to produce a horizontal body position and an efficient kick will be used instead simply to control trim.

Jack Benedick, of Littleton, Colorado, Competition Director of the National Handicapped Sports and Recreation Association, and a scuba instructor, offers the following observations for other amputees. A single above-the-knee amputee should avoid using a prosthetic with a knee made of metal susceptible to saltwater corrosion. Instead, the amputee might wear a wooden or otherwise waterproof peg leg attached to the prosthetic socket. To facilitate walking on the boat or beach, the peg leg should equalize the length of the legs. Fins can be attached to the peg leg, perhaps with a combination of Velcro and other fasteners. Alternatively, the fin can mount on a prosthetic foot that screws directly

A diver assembles his prosthetics.

Without proper buoyancy in the prostheses, a diver struggles to achieve proper trim.

into the socket. The peg leg then would only be used to walk on the boat or beach.

A single below-the-knee amputee can simply mount a fin directly on the prosthetic socket because the difference in length of the legs is not significant enough to unbalance the swim.

Jack himself is a bilateral below-the-knee amputee and is delighted with the prostheses the Veterans Administration had made for him. Manufactured from space-age materials, the prostheses have waterproof drop ankles. A quick-release pin holds the foot in a walking position. After donning the fins and entering the water, Jack pulls the pin and the foot flattens into a swimming position.

The Gadget

The Gadget, as it has been dubbed for lack of a better name, is an invention that holds a diver's console, containing underwater gauges, within view throughout a dive. This eliminates the need to reach for the console with a hand otherwise engaged. As the diver swims along, the pressure gauge, depth gauge, bottom timer, compass, watch, thermometer, and so forth can be constantly monitored because the console stays in place parallel to the diver's body, in front of the face. Because the console is long and narrow, it does not noticeably impair the diver's vision. The diver does not need his or her hands to find, transport, or hold the console. This feature makes the Gadget an indispensable tool for divers whose arms are kept busy with swimming and maintaining orientation.

Divers who swim with their arms must break the pace of their swim in order to pull a console up from their sides. If the console is large enough to hold a number of gauges, it is also large enough to create a considerable drag as the diver moves it to a position where it can be read. This drag can be enough to upset the delicate balance the diver has established to maintain body orientation in the water (see "Trim"). Often when body orientation is lost, buoyancy control is lost, too. The diver may complete the gauge check only to discover that body orientation and buoyancy must be reestablished. Even in instances where body orientation and buoyancy are not lost in this process, repeated interruptions of the swim to check gauges are irritating and time consuming.

A more serious dilemma is caused by the occasional need to swim with two hands while holding a compass steady with two hands. There are just not enough hands to go around. The compass, to guide navigation effectively, must be held constantly. It is not practical to hold the compass, put it down and swim for a bit, then stop swimming to pull the compass back again. Attempting to do this is particularly distressing when the diver sees nothing but silt and must also monitor depth constantly.

The Gadget solves these problems. Two versions have been developed to date. The first is essentially a harness made of two flexible shoulder straps running from the chest over the shoulders to the shoulder blades, with a chest strap circling the body and running through holders at the ends of the shoulder straps. Weight-belt webbing is used for the straps. The holders are mounted on a light aluminum bar at the front and back that also separates the shoulder straps. The front bar provides a place to mount the arm that holds the console. Also a bar of light aluminum, this arm can be bent to the exact angle that provides optimum viewing of the console.

The Gadget is a harness that holds the diver's console.

A more packable and only slightly less secure version omits the harness and attaches with Velcro directly to the jacket BCD. The arm holding the console is identical to that used in the harness version but attaches instead to a simple cross made of two lightweight aluminum bars. A long bar (about 8 to 10 inches in length would be comfortable for divers with a medium to large frame) crosses horizontally and a shorter bar (about 6 or 7 inches) crosses vertically. The horizontal bar is covered with Velcro on the outside (the side facing the arm). Matching Velcro is affixed to the inside of each side of the BCD at the chest, where the BCD will close over the Gadget when the Gadget is positioned correctly. The vertical bar prevents the Gadget from moving up and down or toward or away from the face.

This model of the Gadget has several advantages. It fits more easily into a gear bag and is less cumbersome to tote around. More importantly, when used in conjunction with the Aqua-Caddy console (see photo below), it can be mounted on the console while entering and exiting the water. After an entry or before an exit, the diver simply attaches or unattaches the Gadget from the Velcro on the BCD. This saves the diver the bother of putting on and taking off an additional piece of equipment at the staging area. When seas are rough and gear should be removed and passed up quickly, this is a real asset. By contrast, to use the harness-type Gadget, a diver puts the harness on under the BCD jacket. After a diver has entered the water, the console is placed in the holder on the arm. Divers who exit facing the platform or ladder must

The Gadget enables the diver to use a compass and monitor her gauges without stopping her swim.

remove the harness and pass it up before leaving the water to avoid snaring the arm.

To date two different methods exist by which the console is placed in the arm. With the first, a hollow tube several inches long is attached to the bottom of the arm. A Pelican-style console is mounted on a plate that attaches to a smaller tube that fits inside the tube on the arm. A pop-out, quick-lock mechanism in the tube, such as the one used to adjust the length of crutches or pool-cleaning poles, holds the console in place. This style requires good manual dexterity and can be difficult to use for divers with weak fingers or divers wearing thick wetsuit mitts. With the second version of the Gadget, a V-shaped holder replaces the tube at the end of the arm and an Aqua-Caddy console, with its V-shaped end, slips easily into place. No locking mechanism is needed with this style.

If the diver needs to move the console out of the way, as might be the case when swimming through a very small space or when using diver rescue techniques, the console can be removed from its holder in the harness and left to trail behind as any console would, or, with the second version, the entire Gadget can be removed from the BCD and left in place on the console.

With the compass mounted directly on the console and the console in place on the harness, the compass will be level only when the diver is in a horizontal position. More flexibility in the diver's positioning while using the compass is possible with a liquid-filled compass in which the dial and needle float a bit inside the case. Even with this sort of compass, the diver cannot take readings while in a vertical position at the surface without removing the console from the Gadget. To avoid this necessity, the diver can mount a compass with a side window (which permits the diver to take a reading by looking into a side wall as well as by looking down on the face) on a hinge that is in turn mounted on the console. The hinge should be of nonmagnetic material and be stiff enough to stay in place when adjusted without falling back into the fully closed or fully open position. This enables the diver to position the compass and then free the hands to maintain orientation in the water. When the diver is on the surface, the compass can be flipped up perpendicular to the console and readings can be taken through the side window. When the diver returns to a horizontal position underwater, the compass is tilted back down so it lays flat and face up on the console.

Because the console cannot be rotated in the Gadget, all instruments must be mounted on the front of the console. With the Aqua-Caddy console, a slate attached to the back of the console can be

The compass is tilted up at the surface to take bearings through its side window.

accessed by removing the console from the arm, reversing it, and using it either while it's free or after replacing it backwards in the arm. The most convenient way to mount a slate on a Pelican console is to install it on the back of the console so that it can pivot out to the side. Divers can then write on the side of the slate that faces inward.

The Gadget is not currently manufactured commercially. Although this means that divers must build their own Gadgets, it also presents the possibility that any diver may develop a more effective design. If you build a good Gadget, we would like to hear from you.

Tanks

Although the type of tank a diver uses is unlikely to affect diving greatly, several factors may make things more or less convenient. These factors include the amount of air the tank holds and its weight, size, buoyancy, boot, and valve.

The primary consideration in selecting a tank is to make sure the diver will have enough air to maximize bottom time. The amount of air a tank holds affects its size and weight. An aluminum tank that holds only 50 cubic feet of air (a 50) is much shorter and lighter than an aluminum tank that holds 80 cubic feet of air (an 80). Similarly, a steel 94 holds a lot more air but is a little bigger and much heavier than a steel 72. An aluminum 80 is a little taller than a steel 72, weighs a bit more, and holds more air. The new stainless steel tank (which at the time of this writing has been advertised but not manufactured and delivered) offers more air for less weight in both the 89- and 75-cubic-foot sizes, but unfortunately they are advertised at twice the price of conventional tanks. Divers who are able to carry their own equip-

Table 1 Comparison of Tank Specifications

Metal	Size (cu ft[1])	PSI	Length (inches)	Diameter (inches)	Weight (lbs)	Buoyancy Full	Empty (lbs)
Alum	100	3300	29.25	8.00	42.32	−4.90	+2.40
Alum	80	3000	29.25	7.25	33.2	−2.20[3]	+3.80[3]
Alum	63	3000	25.10	7.25	28.4	−3.04	+1.69
Alum	50	3000	22.25	6.90	23.0	−2.60	+1.04
Steel	72[2]	2250	28.25	6.90	31.5	−5.40[3]	0[3]
Steel	94[2]	3300	25.00	7.00	39.0		−6.00
Stnls	89[2]	3300	25.25	7.25	29.0		+1.00
Stnls	75[2]	3300	25.50	7.25	24.3		+1.00

Comparison of Weight, Air Capacity, and Buoyancy for Doubles

	Weight (lbs)	Capacity (cu ft)	Buoyancy (empty)
Alum 80s	66.4	154.8	+8.12
Steel 72s	63.0	142.4[2]	0[3]
Stnls 89s	58.0	177.8[2]	+2.00
Alum 63s	56.8	126.0	+3.38
Stnls 75s	48.6	149.4[2]	+2.00
Alum 50s	46.0	97.0	+2.08

[1]The true cubic foot capacity of some tanks differs from that suggested by its name. The aluminum 50 holds 48.5 cubic feet of air, the 63 holds 63, the 80 holds 77.4, the steel 72 holds 71.2, the steel 94 holds 94.6, the stainless steel 75 holds 74.7, and the stainless steel 89 holds 88.9. Capacity of doubles was figured using the true cubic foot capacity.
[2]Capacity for the steel and stainless steel tanks has been figured including the 10% overfill that is allowed only when the tanks meet certain rigorous criteria.
[3]This information is taken from the National Speleogical Society's Cave Diving Manual instead of the retailers' charts as is the rest. Information provided by retailers suggests that the aluminum 80 is 4.1 pounds positive when empty and that the steel 72 is 3.5 pounds positive when empty. (See, for example, Dacor's promotional material.) The experience of divers who have used both tanks indicates that the difference between the two is greater than these figures suggest and that the steel 72 is closer to neutral when empty.

Note. The information in this table was compiled in part from the *Cave diving manual* (p. 65), by the National Speleological Society, Venice, FL: Author; and the Cylinder Comparison Chart from Dacor Corporation, Northfield, Illinois. Reprinted with permission.

ment may want to consider their ability to lift and carry a tank when deciding which tank to use. Table 1 compares specifications for various tanks commonly available.

Some divers may need to consider the buoyancy of various tanks and the fact that their buoyancy increases as the air supply is depleted. A steel 72 is about 5.4 pounds negatively buoyant when full and neutrally buoyant when empty; an aluminum 80 is about 2.2 pounds negatively buoyant when full and 3.8 pounds positively buoyant when empty. This means that the diver must add positive buoyancy at the beginning of a dive with a steel tank (by adding air to the BCD only when needed) and negative buoyancy at the end of a dive with an aluminum tank (by permanently adding 3 or 4 pounds to the weight belt). If a diver's need to minimize the amount of weight on the weight belt exceeds the need to maximize the air supply, 3 or 4 pounds can be omitted by using the steel 72 instead of the aluminum 80. Most divers, however, find the aluminum 80 has the most advantages with the fewest disadvantages.

Divers who don their tanks sitting down will notice a big difference between the short 50 and tall tanks such as the 72 or the 80 in the positioning of the BCD on the tank when they slip it on. For divers with limited trunk strength who cannot support the tank's weight while they sit with it on at the water's edge, the length of the tank makes a difference in the gearing-up process. A tank that rests on the deck when properly mounted on the back of a seated diver is much easier to handle than a short tank and may even provide some support when the deck is not rolling. A jacket BCD can be positioned carefully on the tank to optimize orientation in the water (see "Trim"). To get into it, the diver stands it up on the pool edge or dive platform and sits in front of it to put it on. If the placement of the jacket on the tank is higher than where students wear it, they will be unable to get up into it. If the jacket is held lower than where students wear it, its weight will pull them over. In either case, they will be unable to adjust the straps properly before entering the water. Unless a student has a very short torso, a 50 is usually too short. An 80 or a 72 is usually a good size for a student of average height. The new aluminum 63, which is about 4 inches shorter than the 80 and about 3 inches taller than the 50, may work well for smaller divers.

Steel tanks have a rounded bottom. Boots are placed on the bottom of the tank to provide a flat surface on which the tank can stand. A boot providing a high degree of stability should be selected by those who will put their tanks on sitting down.

Experienced divers may want to select different tanks for different purposes. For example, divers may prefer the lightweight con-

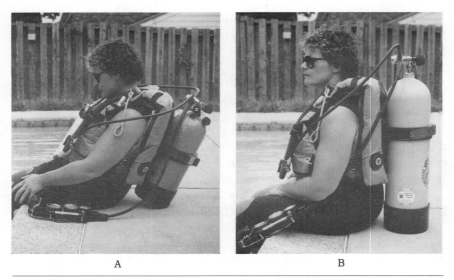

A   B

Divers of average height must slump over to fit in the BCD assembled on a 50 (photo A), but can sit normally when donning an 80 (photo B).

venience of a 50 in warm, shallow water when they know air consumption will be low. The same divers may want to use an aluminum 100 or two 80s or 72s joined together as doubles when diving in deep, cold water when they know air consumption will be higher, and more air is needed for a safety margin.

Tanks are available with either J or K valves. J valves were vitally important before air pressure gauges became available because their "300 pound reserve" function, when working properly, provided divers with their only warning that air was almost exhausted and that it was time to surface. Flipping the J mechanism down allowed the diver to use this last 300 pounds for the ascent. The problem with the J valve is that it can malfunction or be accidentally deactivated during a dive, providing no warning that the air supply has been depleted. Now that air pressure gauges are available, using so imprecise and unreliable a system is unnecessary. In any event, divers with limited range of motion in the shoulder, with limited manual dexterity, or with the tank positioned low in the jacket BCD will be unable to reach back to the tank valve to activate the reserve air supply unless it is equipped with a pull rod running down the length of the tank. All divers must learn to monitor the air pressure gauge constantly and always to be aware of the air supply remaining in the tank. The K valve gives the diver access to the entire air supply without having to activate a reserve. Used in conjunction with the air pressure gauge, this is a simpler, more accurate, and more reliable system than reliance on the J valve.

The on/off knob on the air supply valve of a tank may determine how easily it is used. Some knobs are short and stubby and rather difficult to manipulate even with good manual dexterity. Several models of knobs are available that provide a much easier grip. A student should try operating the valve before selecting a tank.

Wet Suits

Much to the chagrin of all divers, wet suits cannot be avoided in any but the warmest of waters. Divers with weak leg or arm muscles find getting into wet suits one of diving's big challenges. Minimizing the time and effort required for this process is well worth careful planning and possible expense.

The type of material used for a wet suit has a lot to do with how easily it pulls on. The fabric from which wet suits are made has changed over the years from solid rubber to rubber on one side and nylon or

The valve on the tank on the right is difficult to operate even with optimal manual dexterity; the valve on the tank on the left is easier to operate.

another synthetic fabric on the other side; to blown nitrogen neoprene with fabric on both sides; to the latest super-supple materials. The earlier style suits, with a rubber side against the skin, provide the greatest thermal protection but unfortunately are the most difficult to put on. This difficulty can be eased, but not eliminated, by sprinkling corn starch, unscented talcum powder, or soapy water inside the wet suit. Suits with a fabric liner on both sides do not bind against the skin and slide on more easily. The early versions of this kind of suit, which are still on the market, are very stiff, making them a bit difficult to put on. The new supple wet suits, made of plush fabric, are soft and very easy to put on. Some of these new suits, however, are extremely buoyant, requiring the diver to wear an impractically large amount of weight. When selecting a wet suit, the diver should balance the need for thermal protection, the ease with which the material can be pulled on, and the buoyancy of the suit.

Any wet suit can be made easier to put on by adding zippers. Some commercially available wet suits have a number of zippers over gussets so that before the zippers are zipped, the wet suit is as loosely fitting and easy to put on as regular clothes. When the zippers are zipped, the gussets fold under and the suit becomes tight. Zippers can be added to a regular wet suit to achieve the same result. Thought should be given to the placement and direction of zippers to allow easy access by the diver or a helper. The addition of zippers will cause some loss of thermal protection, but for most divers, this loss is outweighed by the greatly increased ease of use.

A new kind of dive suit appropriate for warm water has recently become available. It is a full-length body suit made of lycra or lycra and nylon and is said to permit the diver to tolerate water 6 degrees cooler than without the suit. Even though experience does not support this claim, the suit is advantageous in tropical water because it protects the skin against coral scrapes, jellyfish stings, and similar hazards. Worn under some types of wet suits, it allows the suit to slip on far more easily and adds extra thermal protection.

Regulators and Octopuses

Divers with reduced lung power may find that the "easy breathing" regulators save them enough effort to make a difference in how tired they feel toward the end of a dive. Dive shop staff may assure a cus-

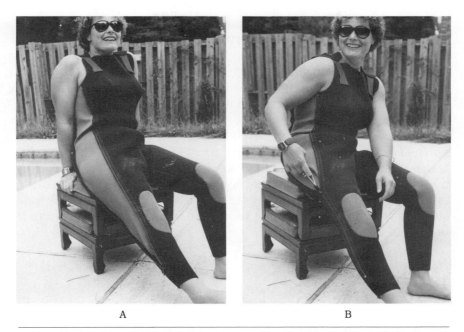

A B

A diver slips into her wet suit easily when zippers allow the gusset underneath to open out (photo A) and zips it up before entering the water (photo B).

tomer that each regulator breathes easily, but they may do so only because they have enough lung power that they do not notice differences in breathability. The top model or top few models in most regulator manufacturers' lines are usually easy breathing regulators. The Navy conducts tests to compare various regulators, and the results are periodically published in *Undercurrents*, a diving newsletter.

Divers with limited manual dexterity and arm strength can make sharing air off their primary regulators easier by using a regulator with the exhaust port on the end (Poseidon 300 and Tekna regulators have this feature). This avoids the necessity of keeping the regulator upright in order to purge the water before inhaling.

Divers with limited use of the hands and arms who find it difficult to roll over and retrieve their regulators (or students who have not yet mastered the skill) may want to consider using a neck strap attached to the regulator. The neck strap that several manufacturers once provided with their regulators attached to the base of the mouthpiece, fitted around the neck, and snapped back onto itself. Any method of holding the mouthpiece where the diver can easily retrieve it if it falls or is knocked out of the mouth can be equally effective. Using any type of device to hold the mouthpiece makes air sharing from the primary regulator virtually impossible in an emergency and should be avoided unless the diver has an octopus.

A second regulator mouthpiece, often called an octopus, is an important piece of equipment for any safety-conscious diver. For divers who perform all diving tasks with their arms, an octopus is essential (see "Buddy Breathing"). Because divers who swim with their arms need more space between themselves and their buddies, a 5-foot hose on their octopus is a real convenience. (The extra hose should be secured along the side of the BCD so it does not dangle down, stirring up silt or getting caught on rocks or pieces of wreck.) Divers who can't afford to keep their hands busy for long will want to use an alligator clip or a loop of surgical tubing to keep the octopus in place where it is easy to reach.

Lights

Soon after their basic class, many students who have become enthusiastic about diving take an advanced class. Most of these classes include night diving, and the student learns the proper use of underwater lights. Divers who swim with their arms do not carry lights in their hands. If they did, the light would simply follow the wide swing of their hands, never shining where needed unless the diver stopped swimming to point the light. These divers mount the lights in one or more locations on their bodies or gear.

A few helmets that hold one or more lights, as miners' helmets do, are commercially available. A less expensive alternative is simply to attach a light in some safe and reliable fashion. The most effective location for a light is on the top of the head. With this arrangement, the light is already shining wherever the diver looks. One light that is particularly well suited for this system is the Underwater Kinetics series of Q lights. Velcro straps can be substituted for the straps that come with the holster for the Q light. The matching Velcro strips can be glued on a wet suit hood in a position that allows the light to shine where the eyes focus. The straps should be positioned while the diver wears the hood and holds the light in its holster, experimenting with different positioning options. When the straps are glued on, the hood should be stretched over the head or any object resembling the size and shape of the owner's head (a balloon or ball). For warm-water diving, the light is best attached to a loose-fitting, thin hood or a

The Q light properly mounted on the diver's hood will always be shining where she is looking.

The Q light comes with an optional holster. Velcro straps through the holster, matched with Velcro straps on a diver's hood, hold the light in place on the head.

leather bicycle helmet, and for cold-water diving it is attached to the diver's wet suit hood. When this light is used as the diver's primary light, the most powerful, longest lasting Q light, the rechargeable Super QXL, is recommended.

Tekna now offers "The I-Beam," a headlight that snaps onto certain of their masks. It is reported to have 12,000 candlepower and to provide a continuous white light for 90 minutes. (By contrast, the rechargeable Super Q has 35,000 candlepower.) This light may be useful, if not as a primary light, at least as a handy backup.

If more light is needed than a Q light emits, larger lights can be attached to the diver's body or gear. For example, an Ikelite C light may be used. This light comes with an optional holster. If the holster's straps are rotated 90 degrees, it can be worn on a weight belt or BCD belt, again leaving the hands free. Because the holster will slide off the belt when the gear is removed, the light should be clipped to the BCD or weight belt. The disadvantage of this system is that the light shines below the diver no matter where the diver wants to look.

Another alternative, providing a far more powerful light to shine ahead of the diver, is to use an Underwater Kinetics 1200 rechargeable light (the UK600R and UK1200 may also be used, but they are less powerful lights). This is a large and, unfortunately, heavy cylindrical light with a removable handle. If the handle is removed and a harness rigged around the light, the harness can be attached to the BCD so that the light hangs down parallel to the diver and shines ahead. Because it will normally be rigged in the dark and in an awkward, upright position, the method of attaching the light should be very simple.

Many other lights can be rigged in some way to be worn rather than held by a diver. For example, a small light may be mounted to the Gadget if the diver uses one. Factors to consider in selecting a light to be worn on the body or gear include where the diver wants the light to shine (straight ahead or straight down), how much light is needed, the weight and buoyancy of the light, how easy the light is to mount, and how much drag it will create.

No matter where or how a diver mounts lights, at least one light must be mounted in such a way that it can be moved around enough to produce signals such as the "I'm okay" and "Distress" signals. Both the Q light mounted on a hood and the C light worn on a belt are positioned flexibly enough to permit effective signalling.

Even with one or more primary lights attached to the body, divers should consider keeping another small light in the BCD pocket. This light can be used on an as-needed basis when the primary is not shining in the right direction and during the day to explore the many small

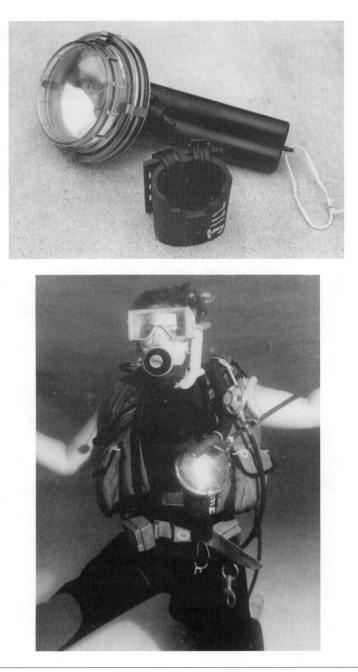

The C light also comes with an optional holster that can be worn on a BCD strap or weight belt.

This diver is laying a line by swimming along with the handle of the line reel tucked into her BCD strap.

A diver can free one hand momentarily while reeling in a line by holding the turn crank and the handle with one hand.

underwater holes or crevices. Because it may be turned on and off frequently, an on/off switch that can be operated with one hand is a real convenience on this spare light.

Line Reels

Experienced divers with special training sometimes find themselves in circumstances requiring the use of a line that is laid from a line reel. Unfortunately there is not yet a one-handed line reel. Although this makes using a line reel by divers who do it all with their arms somewhat impractical, a few considerations make its use a bit easier.

If the line reel has a long, solid handle that can be quickly and easily tucked under a belt, line can be laid by tucking the reel into the belt and swimming along. Alternately, the line reel may be attached to a diver with a snap hook. In either case, the reel should have a braking mechanism to keep tension on the line while it is laid.

The turn-handle that reels the line back in should be large enough and positioned in such a way that the thumb can hold it in place while the rest of the hand holds the reel's handle. This frees the other hand periodically.

The line reel should be as small as possible, given the amount of line needed. Because it is tucked in a belt or attached by a snap hook when line is being laid, the reel is susceptible to banging and catching on objects beneath the diver. The smaller the reel, the less of a problem this will be.

The line chosen for the line reel should reflect the fact that divers who propel themselves with their arms pull themselves along the line when reeling it in. Divers should select a line that is strong enough to withstand this additional stress.

Lift Bags

Experienced divers use lift bags to bring submerged objects to the surface. Lift bags are available with or without deflate cords. Adjusting ones without deflate cords requires the use of two hands and a lot of time to tilt the bag sidewise to let the proper amount of air escape. Adjusting lift bags with the deflate cord requires only one hand to let air out, and the other hand is needed only momentarily (if at all) to steady the lift bag. Divers whose hands are always busy will want to use a lift bag with a deflate cord.

Skills

Skills *3*

Water Skills Evaluation

During the first training session in the pool, scuba instructors evaluate their students' water skills, as their training agencies often require. Common requirements are (a) swimming 220 yards on the surface without stopping, using any stroke; (b) staying afloat for twenty minutes using any combination of techniques; and (c) swimming 20 yards underwater. In addition to measuring the students' fitness, these requirements help the instructor evaluate the students' confidence, comfort level, and general abilities in the water.

It goes without saying that it is equally important for instructors to evaluate disabled students this way. And as they are with non-disabled students, instructors must be ready and willing to act upon the results. Like other students, disabled students lacking the necessary water skills can be invited to return to the scuba class after they have developed them. The seas are no more forgiving because a diver has a disability.

Many disabled students have no more difficulty with the swimming requirements than do other students. Even students with no use of their legs can often meet the technical requirements outlined above if they have good upper body strength and range of motion. Students without these advantages may cover the same distance more slowly but often with no difficulty. As with other students, disabled students who are out of shape are not able to perform at or near their maximum ability. As it is the case sometimes for other students, these students can be allowed to get in shape by the end of the course.

A few disabled students may not, even when in shape, be able to perform the technical swimming requirements but still may have the water skills necessary for safe diving. Many experienced instructors find that they can assess fitness and water skills without testing for the prescribed swimming skills and do so in a more informal water exercise session. These instructors have no problem assessing the needed qualities and skills in students who do not meet the technical requirements. A relaxed or anxious face looks the same on any tired swimmer no matter how much swimming was done. The puffing and panting of a swimmer who has swum underwater for a distance greater than was comfortable looks the same even though that distance might be less than that for other swimmers. Instructors can thus judge any student's ability to handle stresses that may arise while diving.

Instructors who usually use the swimming skill requirements suggested by their training agencies should consider how a disability affects the accomplishment of each requirement and the extent to which that requirement is a predictor of a student's potential to become a safe diver. For example, disabilities that weaken leg muscles so that they provide no useful kick while swimming affect the speed at which students swim. In timed exercises, such as the underwater distance swim, these students will be at a disadvantage. Although they may be able to hold their breaths as long as equally fit, kicking swimmers, they will not cover the same distance laterally underwater (even though they may easily cover the same distance in the same time on an ascent). Before disqualifying such students, instructors should consider whether the inability to swim that distance underwater really means that the student cannot become a safe diver. If it does not, and if their training agency permits it, instructors should consider substituting a requirement that makes sense in the circumstances.

As in the case of any other student, the bottom line in evaluating a disabled student's basic aquatic ability is the instructor's professional opinion of that individual's potential safety in the water.

Equipment Preparation

Divers who use wheelchairs and have good upper body strength and manual dexterity often find they are able to lug around their gear by putting a tank between their legs on the footplates and the gear bag and/or another tank on their laps. This only works on fairly flat, level, hard surfaces. Because scuba gear, essentially weightless underwater, can be a burden for anyone on the way to the water's edge, divers of all ability levels assist each other with gear transport and other chores of sport diving. Divers unable to transport gear need only to pitch in in the manner and to the extent they are able. Nevertheless, each individual is still responsible for ensuring that his or her gear has reached its destination and for soliciting whatever assistance is needed to complete the job.

Divers who use wheelchairs on land often carry their tanks on their footplates and their gear on their laps.

Students with limited manual dexterity normally need help assembling their BCD, tank, and regulator. It is a good idea to have another instructor or an assistant instructor provide this assistance. The student must learn how the gear is assembled and watch the assistant carefully to make sure everything is done properly. When the air is turned on, the student should check the pressure gauge. Like commercial hard-hat divers who are suited up by a tender, sport divers who need assistance should not abdicate responsibility for their own safety. After the student has mastered these skills and gained confidence in their use, the instructor or assistant instructor should purposely make errors in assembly to be sure the student has learned the process and always pays careful attention.

Students with limited manual dexterity will also need assistance assembling the weights and weight belt. Placement of the weights on the weight belt is very important to these students, so it is important that they learn where the weights should be and how to explain to the assistant where to place them and how to secure them.

These students will also likely need help assembling the mask and snorkle and, once in the water, assembling the console and the Gadget (see "The Gadget") if one is used. Again, students should learn how to tell an assistant exactly what needs to be done.

The instructor or assistant might have an impulse to simply do these tasks for the student to avoid the drudgery of talking through it. All parties should consider that the student may be certified, go on a diving vacation, sign onto a large charter boat, and end up being assisted by a buddy with rusty diving skills. In such situations, there is no place for unnecessary dependency.

Equipment Donning

There is only one practical way for people who can't support the weight of the tank on their back while standing to don their gear on land. That is to put on everything that that person can handle while mobile, move the rest of the gear to one spot at the very edge of the pool (dock, boat, or beach), sit down, and put on the rest of the gear there. Once the gear is on, the diver simply falls (or scoots) into the water.

The key to the success of this system is that it is done at the exact point the diver will be entering the water. The individual who cannot support the weight of the tank while standing also cannot put it on while seated and then get back up to move to the stern or anywhere else. Therefore, when boat diving, this gearing up occurs on the dive platform or at that point on the transom or gunnel where the diver enters the water. At pools, beaches, or docks it occurs anywhere the diver can enter the water. Because some gearing up will be done in the limited area available on the dive platform (or other entry point), the process should be efficient so the staging in of other divers is not delayed.

Until students learn to gear up quickly, they may want to consider letting other divers who do gear up more quickly stage in first. The easiest way to cut time from the gearing-up process is to put on everything possible while still mobile. At the minimum, this should include whatever clothes (including gloves) or wet suit will be worn and the mask and snorkle. Most students who use a Gadget should be able to put it on at this stage. The only exception would be if it interfered with moving to the sitting position. Students who can manage it and who do not use a crotch strap on their BCDs should also put on the weight belt before sitting down at water's edge. Before attempting this, make sure that having on that extra weight will not interfere with the ability to sit down or to transfer from a wheelchair. Remember that it is especially important that the weight belt be securely fastened at the smallest part of the waist. This will leave only the BCD, tank, and regulator assembly to be donned at the entry point. When a student is first learning to don the tank while sitting in front of it or when on a boat shifting with the seas, a buddy should hold the tank secure. Students able to don their gear themselves will quickly learn to wiggle enough to get into the tank without knocking it over. The console is inserted into the Gadget after the diver enters the water.

Note that once the student is sitting down, there is no getting up again without taking off the gear. For this reason, if the student's buddy gears up in the traditional standing-up method, the buddy should gear up first. While the student is still sitting in a wheelchair, the student can assist the standing buddy. Some divers place their standing buddy's tank on their laps to help the buddy into it. After the standing buddy's tank is donned and the buddy check is complete, the student can sit down and gear up. The standing buddy can do a buddy check at this point.

An alternative to donning the gear at the water's edge or on the boat is to don it in the water. This method is not practical for boat diving in any but the calmest seas or for beach entries where there is a

A diver dons her tank sitting at the water's edge.

The wheelchair user helps her buddy gear up while she is still seated in her chair.

surf. It is taught only as an alternative for either students who cannot make an entry geared up or for other students to use in calm water. With this method, the student can don whatever is convenient at water's edge, such as T-shirt, gloves, mask and snorkle, and the Gadget and then enter the water. The BCD is donned, followed by the weight belt. Unless the diver has enough buoyancy from a wet suit to compensate for the weight on a weight belt, the latter should *never* be donned before the BCD. Without a strong kick, the student will rely on the BCD for whatever buoyancy is needed to compensate for weight.

Students who can gear up themselves and who use their gear and arms for stability in the water normally find this method more difficult. Putting on the weight belt, for example, requires both hands and leaves the student unable to maintain stability in the water. For students who need assistance donning their gear, this method may be easier because it is easier for the assistant to get under and around the student in the water.

Some students, particularly those with limited manual dexterity and upper body strength, will need assistance donning their gear. As with assembling gear, it is the student's responsibility to learn what help is needed and how to describe it to their buddy or other assistant.

Her buddy helps her gear up as she sits at the water's edge.

An especially vexing task in the gearing-up process is getting legs that don't flex and a bottom that is being sat upon into wet suit pants or a farmer john. The section on wet suits (see "Wet Suits") suggests some types of modifications that make the process easier. Lacking these, tricks like using corn starch or warm soapy water or one of the new Lycra body suits should be used. If a student who uses a wheel-chair needs assistance getting into pants or a farmer john, it may be easiest to have an assistant push the wet suit legs up to the knees from the front of the student. Then two assistants stand on either side of the student and pull the wet suit as high up on the thighs as possible. To fit it over the hips, the two assistants stand the student up and slide the wet suit up to the waist. The rest is elementary.

Water Entries

The most common method of entering the water from a pool edge or pier for people who don't stand with their gear on is to sit on the edge fully geared and roll into the water. Before entering the water,

A diver's buddy helps him into his wet suit.

While he's still seated, the wet suit is pulled up midthigh.

As he supports himself on their shoulders, they pull the wet suit up.

the student should add enough air to the BCD to hold the head above water. The student should hold the mask and regulator secure with one hand and gauges with the other. The student should take care when rolling into the water to make sure that the tank will clear the lip on the pool's edge without getting caught. Early in the training, a student without the upper body strength to stay upright in the water may not be wearing a properly fitted BCD. If this is the case, the buddy should enter the water first and be prepared to provide stability.

Students who are able to support some of the weight of the tank can roll over forward into the water. If the student prefers, a sidewise twist can be added so the shoulder hits the water first. Some students may find it easier to sit sideways on the edge and fall in on their side.

Students who are able to support the weight of the tank hanging over the water can turn around and do an ordinary back roll. If possible, the legs should be crossed over each other, the gauges should lie in the lap, and the hand that is not holding the mask secure should hold the legs during the entry. This entry is preferred by those who can do it when dropping into the water from a height.

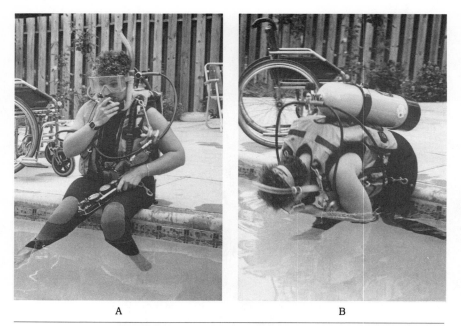

A   B

For a front-roll entry, the diver sits at the edge of the pool, pier, boat, or platform (photo A), leans forward, and rolls in (photo B).

A diver prepares for a back-roll entry. This entry requires strong trunk muscles and good balance.

The back roll can provide a more comfortable landing than a front roll.

Boats

Boat entries use whatever version of the rollover is most convenient, given the boat's configuration. If the boat has a dive platform, it is often easiest to put on the tank there and roll forward into the water. If the seas are so rough that water pushes the student around on the platform, an entry from the gunnel may be safer and easier. Students may need help staying balanced on the gunnel as they gear up and prepare to fall in. Any entry that successfully and safely lands the student and gear intact and in the water is a good entry.

Beaches Without Surf

Beach entries almost always involve a good bit of dragging along in the muck or sand. The diver approaches water's edge and puts assembled gear and self in the deepest water that can easily be reached without soaking the wheelchair. Sitting there the diver gears up and, when ready, begins to inch out into deeper and deeper water until floating free. The wet suit, gauges, regulators, and so on collect a lot of particulate matter during this process. The student should make a special effort to remember to check the regulator again before going down and then to rinse gear thoroughly after diving.

Beaches With Surf

Beaches with surf offer an even more challenging entry. It is often easiest, after donning the gear sitting at water's edge, to scoot backwards into deeper water. As waves rush toward the beach, divers hold their position. When the waves wash outward again, divers take advantage of that force to move them further into the water. The usual precautions to avoid lung overinflation when a wave washes over the diver must be observed.

Trim

One of the most important functions strong legs perform in diving is providing balance and orientation in the water, keeping both the head constant relative to the feet and the body from rolling side to side. Divers who don't have strong legs use the careful placement of weight to achieve orientation and balance. Determining the proper placement and amount of weight must be accomplished early in the dive training. Until it has been worked out properly, students will spend much of their time and effort struggling to achieve and maintain the desired position in the water. Consequently, students compromise attention to other tasks, such as mask clearing, buddy breathing, or regulator retrieval. Additionally, without proper trim, propulsion is both difficult and inefficient. Orientation drills, in which students practice achieving and maintaining proper orientation in the water without side-to-side roll and without significant changes in head-to-toe positioning, should be practiced early and often. The importance of proper trim to pleasurable diving cannot be overemphasized.

Side-to-Side Roll

The tendency to roll side to side is controlled by careful placement of weights on the weight belt. As a general rule, students will be more stable in the water if they wear their weight close to the buckle of the weight belt. Placing the weight here counterbalances the weight of the tank, which otherwise tends to pull a diver over on the back. The weights should be evenly distributed on each side to avoid rolling the diver to one side. The weight belt should be snug enough that it will not flop around at depth. If this cannot be achieved with a traditional weight belt, a compressible weight belt should be used (see "Weight Belt"). Clips on either side of the weights (weight-belt keepers) or twists in the weight belt itself should be used to keep the weights from shifting once the diver enters the water.

Weights can be purposefully placed off center to compensate for a student's tendency to roll in either direction. For example, a student whose legs always spasm in a way that rolls the body over on the right side can place more weight on the left side. Whatever placement of weight that keeps the diver comfortable and stable in the prone position is the right placement.

Approaching a Straight Posture

Legs without strong muscles to keep them rigid behind a diver tend to bend at the hips and knees and float in a variety of directions. The main principle in achieving stability along the head-to-toe plane is simply to weight whatever floats too high and to add buoyancy to whatever sinks too low. Students generally start practicing trim in the

Swimming at a 45° angle is a lot of work.

Swimming on a level plane, at least from shoulders to knees, is much easier.

pool, wearing no wet suit. It is not uncommon to see students with knees sinking well below the plane of their shoulders and hips, while their feet float either straight behind the knees or somewhat higher. It will often be difficult and is unnecessary to get both the knees and the feet on the same plane as the shoulders and hips. Getting the knees up to hip level will keep them from dragging on the bottom and will create a more efficient swimming position. Even if the feet float up perpendicularly from the knees, less resistance is created than if the knees sink below the hips. Often, wearing wet suit booties or sneakers will add enough buoyancy to lift the knees up to hip level. However, this also usually guarantees that the feet will float quite high.

Another option that avoids raising the feet is to use pieces of an old wet suit cut in rectangles large enough to wrap around the knee area. Velcro sewn along the edges will make them easy to put on and take off. If they are large enough and worn directly over the knees, they will also help keep the knees straight. The strips should be no larger than is necessary to bring the knees level with the hips; more will make the legs float too high. The goal is for the student to be straight from shoulders to hips to knees.

Bending at the hips and knees stops when the student dons a wet suit. The stiffness of the neoprene holds legs in a fairly straight position.

Level Head-to-Toe Orientation

Even once the body is straight, the student may tend to point either head up or head down. This will cause the student to work not only for forward propulsion but also for proper orientation in the water. Again, careful placement of weight is the way to avoid wasting all that energy. Where the tank is placed in the backpack has a significant effect on head-to-toe orientation. If the tank is low in the backpack, most of its weight will be low on the student, pushing the lower part of the body down. If the tank is worn high in the backpack, a lot of its weight will be centered over the shoulders, pushing the upper body down. Attention should be paid to helping the student decide where to wear the tank to achieve good head-to-toe orientation. Thought should also be given to the differences between tanks (see "Tanks").

When students are just beginning in the water and it is not desirable to move the tank around in the backpack in the water, or when the tank cannot be placed in such a way as to provide the proper orientation, added weights or buoyancy can be used. Fishing weights attached to alligator clips can be clipped onto whichever end floats too high. They can be moved around easily for optimal weighting. Once optimal weighting has been found using these moveable weights, a more permanent system can be rigged. For example, if weight is needed at the shoulders, pockets can be sewn into the BCD to hold whatever weight is necessary. Because this weight will not be quickly and easily removable in an emergency, it should be the least weight that will be effective and should represent only a small proportion of all weight worn. Alternatively, extra neoprene can be attached where needed for lift. Once a student has had some experience in the water, these fine-tunings are rarely necessary.

When the change from no rubber in the pool to full wet suit in open water occurs, the problem of achieving a comfortable, efficient head-to-toe orientation in the water begins again, only now it is much more complex. When the diver, unaccustomed to the constraints of a wet suit, first jumps into the water, it is a very uncomfortable experience. Inevitably, with all that rubber on the legs, the feet float. On the surface, this tends to push the student over on the back and creates even more discomfort. To make matters worse, descending while in this position is quite a challenge. When air is let out of the BCD, the torso sinks first and the feet follow later. Consequently, the diver is essentially doing a back-over, upside-down dive to descend. This can be disturbing to new students. Many divers who had this experience report that as students they weighted their feet to relieve the discomfort at the surface. The problem is that this solution creates a new problem at depth. What causes the feet to sink 3 or 4 feet at the surface when the wet suit has not compressed will also cause the feet to sink firmly at depth when the suit has compressed. A student weighted to be vertical at the surface will also be vertical at depth. This is worse, despite all the disadvantages of the uncomfortable surface position. A 20- or 30-minute swim in a vertical position is a real workout.

Another alternative for some divers with a lot of upper body strength is to force a rollover onto the stomach and then push the torso up until the body stabilizes in a vertical position. Divers unable to perform this maneuver generally learn to tolerate the surface discomfort, minimize time on the surface, and concentrate on achieving proper head-to-toe orientation at depth. Students who find the discomfort at the surface intolerable can attach moveable weights to their feet at the surface and then remove them, or move them to the center of gravity or to some other spot where they may be needed at depth.

Both the students and instructor should be aware that problems of orientation are exacerbated when the students are wearing wet suits. If students have not paid careful attention to achieving level head-to-toe orientation, they may swim off, unknowingly fighting to stay stable. If they then stop swimming to do a task, such as mask clearing, they will also stop maintaining level orientation. Normally the head will then rise, and they'll become vertical in the water. This will change their buoyancy, and they'll start heading for the surface. While they're still looking for the deflate button, the wet suit will start uncompressing. Before they know it, they'll be looking at the sky. Proper head-to-toe orientation should be achieved before other open-water drills are undertaken.

Every time a student changes the combination of wet suit garments, head-to-toe orientation in the water will change significantly, and the first task in the water should be getting weighted properly to maintain that orientation effortlessly. Although this process is important for all divers, it is critical for divers who rely on weighting to establish proper trim.

Buoyancy Control

Proper weighting and the proficient use of equipment and inflate/deflate procedures, including lung control, become crucial in controlling buoyancy for divers without a strong kick to make up for minor changes and errors.

Students should be weighted so that they will stay firmly planted on the bottom when they empty their BCDs. This will add stability when performing such drills as buddy breathing and equipment ditch and don or when helping a buddy with a slipped tank. On the other hand, students should not be weighted so heavily that they sink more quickly than they can clear their ears.

Students should be careful to remember the effect of wet suit compression when selecting the amount of weight to wear. Extra weight will be needed to overcome the buoyancy of the wet suit in the first 10 to 15 feet before the wet suit compresses. Although this is important on the descent, it is critical on the ascent, when a wet suit's relatively sudden uncompression could cause a dangerously rapid ascent.

Because the greatest relative pressure changes occur at the shallowest depths, minor changes in depth that occur within 15 feet of the surface can cause significant changes in buoyancy. Divers who do not immediately compensate for these changes by kicking need to pay very careful attention to minor buoyancy changes. Frequent adjustments to the amount of air in the BCD are necessary at shallow depths. Students who are not careful to make these minor adjustments before they notice themselves being pulled in one direction or another may be moving much too quickly by the time they find and activate the inflate/deflate button.

Early in their training, students who do it all with their arms should be taught what is often saved for more advanced stages of the training—the effect of lung volume on buoyancy. Students will be able to empty or fill their lungs more quickly than they will be able to find and use their inflate/deflate mechanisms. This effect can lift them as a kick would lift other students who find themselves sinking a little too quickly, for example. Any time a quick change in buoyancy is needed, this technique will buy time until the inflate/deflate mechanism is found and manipulated. The usual precautions to prevent lung overinflation are of utmost importance in using this technique of buoyancy control.

Communication

Manual dexterity is required to make the conventional hand signals used by divers. Students for whom this is not possible should develop their own equivalent signals. The instructor, all pool assistants, and the students' buddies should all learn these signals before anyone enters the water. This may require thinking about underwater communication earlier than usual during the training. Signals need not be limited to what the hands can produce but can include any other purposeful body movements, such as head nods and shakes, shoulder movements, and facial expressions. Students might consider using the latter gestures for signals that are produced frequently, such as "I'm okay."

Although there are no universally accepted signals used by divers without manual dexterity, a few are common. "Up" can be signaled by the relaxed, close-fingered hand pointing up, often accompanied by an upward eye glance for clarity. "Down" is signaled with the opposite gestures. "I'm okay" is often indicated with a nod of the head accompanied by a calm and relaxed facial expression. "Are you okay?" is communicated by that questioning look in the eyes accompanied by a quick upward movement of the head. "I'm not okay" or "I've got a problem" can be signaled with a back and forth movement of the lower arm in a gesture similar to that used by divers communicating distress with an underwater flashlight. It is a good idea for students, instructors, and pool assistants to agree on a separate sign that indicates "I'm not in any distress, but I could use some help."

Divers often attract their buddies' attention by squeezing an arm or leg or tapping on a shoulder. Students who lack feeling in some parts of their bodies should remember to tell their buddies where touching them will be effective.

Students should be reminded throughout the class that when they use signals that differ from the commonly accepted scuba signals, they should teach their signals to each new buddy prior to a dive.

Snorkle and Regulator Use

Students with a restricted range of motion in the arms or with limited manual dexterity may not be able to perform all methods of regulator retrieval. For example, it may be difficult under these circumstances to reach back to the first stage to grab the regulator hose and find the regulator. Even students with complete range of motion and good dexterity have difficulty with this method if they wear their tanks low to achieve their desired orientation in the water. Because there are alternate methods of regulator retrieval, the ability to find it using this method should not dictate tank placement.

All students should be able to retrieve their regulator using at least one method. Most should be able to reach back along the side of the tank to hook the hose and to roll over onto one side so that the second stage falls within reach.

Mask Clearing

Blowing out the water that has seeped (or rushed) into a mask is among the most frequently performed tasks in diving. Divers generally press the mask securely against the forehead with the hand, tilt the head up so the water collects in the bottom of the mask, and blow air into the mask through the nose, pushing the water out. Divers with limited manual dexterity press on the top of the mask with the back of the hand, the palm, the forearm, or whatever else is convenient.

Students who use their arms for propulsion and stability and have not yet mastered the task may find that clearing their masks will disrupt their swimming progress or their orientation. This potential problem normally disappears as soon as mask clearing becomes second nature. At that point, it requires so little time that the fleeting unavailability of one hand does not affect propulsion or stability.

Divers who cannot clear their masks without disrupting their swim even after they have become comfortable in the water should consider using a mask with a purge valve.

Divers with a limited range of motion in the neck that prevents them from tilting their head upwards can clear their masks by tilting the head to either side.

Descents/Ascents

Divers who do not use power to kick into an ascent or to propel them below the surface on a descent use buoyancy control instead.

Descents

Relying only on buoyancy control for a descent requires precise weighting and constant adjustment of the air in the BCD. Divers must carry enough weight that the descent will begin when air is let out of the BCD but not so much weight that they will descend out of control, more quickly than their buddies or than they can clear their ears. Trial and error is the only way to determine the correct amount of weight, but as a general rule, a little more weight is needed than for a diver whose descent is assisted by leg power.

Begin the descent by dumping air from the BCD. Once the descent is underway, the diver should be alert to the need to add small bursts of air to the BCD as the air remaining in the BCD is compressed and provides less buoyancy or when the descent must be slowed. When wearing wet suits, divers must notice the rather sudden change in buoyancy that occurs at about 10 to 15 feet when the wet suit compresses. Air must be added to the BCD to compensate for this significant loss of buoyancy. Learning to add just the right amount of air to the BCD to slow but not reverse a descent is difficult. Students should expect to be rather frustrated in their early efforts to master this skill.

While students are learning to make these fine-tuned adjustments to the BCD, they also must be successfully clearing their ears. When a kick is not available to correct a too-rapid descent during which the ears begin to hurt, adjustments to the BCD will have to be made. Students who do not kick and who have not yet learned to make fine BCD adjustments profit from paying more attention than usual to ear clearing. Because the eustachian tubes respond well to exercise, divers can make their ears easier to clear by practicing clearing them several times a day. On a dive, ear clearing will be easier if the ears are cleared early (before any discomfort is felt) and often.

The usual clearing method divers are taught, by which the nostrils are pinched between thumb and forefinger while air is gently blown against the nose, requires good manual dexterity. An alternative requiring less manual dexterity, using both thumbs for pinching the nostrils, is not desirable because it takes both hands away from the inflate/deflate device, which may then be difficult to relocate. A better alternative is simply to push on the mask with the palm or back of one hand, creating enough pressure in the mask to block the nose effectively. Pushing the skirt of the mask against the nostrils also works for many people.

Some lucky few are able to pop their ears simply by wiggling their jaw, doing a chewing motion, or swallowing. Another method, which takes some practice, is to take a breath of air and while holding it, press the tongue firmly against the roof of the mouth and then sharply and suddenly swallow. For divers who need two hands to control buoyancy, these techniques are invaluable.

Ascents

Ascents present the potential for more serious consequences than the ear-clearing problem associated with too-rapid descents. An ascent that is too rapid can, if done incorrectly, cause a rupture of the air sacs in the lungs and can contribute to the development of decompression sickness. Ascents *must* be controlled to a steady, moderate rate (60 feet per minute or a foot per second is the prescribed rate).

To begin an ascent using buoyancy control, a small amount of air is added to the BCD. Only that amount of air needed to begin the rise should be added. As the ascent proceeds, the air in the BCD will begin to expand, making the diver more buoyant and causing the ascent to become faster and faster. To prevent gathering speed on the ascent, divers must remember to constantly monitor their buoyancy and to let out small bursts of air as the air in the BCD expands. Again, special attention should be paid at about 10 or 15 feet, where the wet suit uncompresses, to avoid shooting to the surface with the added buoyancy.

Students who can operate their inflate button and control their buoyancy with one hand should be able to use the customary procedure on an ascent of tilting the head back, holding one arm up (at least on and off), and slowly turning 360 degrees.

Real-world descents and ascents cannot really be practiced well in a pool only 10 or 12 feet deep. Students will, therefore, do their first real descents and ascents during their open-water checkouts. Because the skills involved take practice to develop and the dangers of a descent or ascent that is too rapid may be serious, the use of a descent/ascent line for the first few direct descents and ascents is recommended. This will give students an opportunity to develop the necessary buoyancy skills in an easily controlled situation.

It is especially important for divers who do not kick to inflate their BCDs immediately upon reaching the surface. It is the BCD that will hold them in a mouth-above-water position. This is more effective than treading, avoids the necessity of expending energy to hold themselves and their gear up in the water, and frees their hands for maintaining stability, switching from regulator to snorkle, making notes on a slate, and so forth.

Using the Lungs

Because divers who do it all with their arms rely heavily on buoyancy control for ascents and descents, it is important that they learn earlier than usual in their training to use control of the amount of air in their lungs to adjust buoyancy. Students can more quickly let some air out of their lungs and breathe shallowly for a short time than they can find and operate the deflate mechanism. This skill should be developed along with the development of buoyancy control using the BCD. In controlling lung volume, divers should *never* hold their breath.

The buoyancy control skills described in this chapter should be developed by every diver seeking maximum safety and comfort in the underwater environment. However, divers without a strong kick should aspire to advanced levels in these skills as part of their basic scuba training.

Propulsion

Divers with some use of their legs should experiment to see whether they can develop any useful propulsion from a kick. Some divers with limited use of one or both legs may find that they can use fins to advantage. (See "Fins" for comments on which fins provide the best advantage for weak legs.) Divers who cannot develop a useful kick with their legs generally do not find any value from fins. Long legs that don't work are difficult enough to control without making them even longer.

Breaststroke

Divers who do not use their legs for propulsion most commonly use a breaststroke to move through the water. By adding a bit of upward or downward movement to this stroke, a diver can control orientation at the same time. A student who needs to improve this stroke can consult any swimming instructor or text. Students and divers who use this stroke should remember to warn each new buddy to keep clear of their arms. This stroke requires more room than divers who kick typically leave between each other. Kicking divers who assume their usual position alongside a diver using the breaststroke will likely lose their mask or regulator early on.

Sculling

Another stroke that can be developed by anyone with strong arms is a sculling stroke done with the arms extended alongside the hips.

A buddy who swims too close to a breaststroking diver may lose his mask or regulator.

The stroke starts with the upper arms at about a 45° angle from the body and the elbows bent so the hands are alongside the hips. With the palms facing out, the forearms push away from the hips until the arms are almost straight. Then the hands turn palm in and the forearms push in toward the body until they are alongside the hips again. This stroke can only be accomplished if the diver's trim is just right, and it cannot be used to help maintain a proper orientation. Sculling is slower than the breaststroke, but it is good for a change, for cruising along a reef, or for any time when speed is unnecessary.

Dog Paddle

A dog paddle-type stroke will also move a diver through the water. This stroke is good for those occasions when a lot of room is not available at the sides for the large sweep of the breaststroke. It is more relaxing than either the breaststroke or the sculling stroke described above. Another significant advantage of the dog paddle is that it can be used to swim a straight line with only one hand. If one hand is pulled down the center of the body, the diver can maintain orientation and move forward through the water. This stroke, therefore, can also be used when one hand is occupied with gear or a buddy or if one hand is injured.

Dolphin Kick

Some divers with neither a strong kick nor a strong arm stroke can get some propulsion using a dolphin kick. In this application, it is less a kick than an undulation down the length of the body that simulates the up-and-down motion of a dolphin swimming. Arms that are not strong enough to produce an effective breaststroke may nevertheless be able to create the movement necessary for this stroke. It begins with the diver horizontal, hands close to the chest. As the arms push simultaneously out and down, the back is arched, pushing the head and chest upward in the water. Then the arms are pulled in toward the hips as the diver bends downward at the waist. The next stroke is not started until the diver feels movement below the waist. The legs should follow, helping to provide the propulsion gained from the undulation. If the strokes are repeated too quickly, the legs will not have time to follow the necessary course and will defeat the entire effort. This stroke must, therefore, be done slowly and almost cautiously until the proper rhythm is established. Although this is not a powerful or fast stroke, it is a restful one and is effective for divers with little upper body strength.

The usual dolphin kick, which relies on the leg(s) to produce the undulation, is used by divers who only have one leg producing a useful kick. Unlike the other kick styles, this kick will produce movement along a straight line even when done with only one leg.

Pulling Along the Bottom

When swimming over a fairly clean wreck or a sandy or rocky bottom, many divers pull themselves along, grabbing the rocks or the solid parts of a wreck or digging a finger or long tool into the sand and pulling. Cave divers and wreck divers often use this pulling technique. The technique can be used by arm-strokers any time there is a clean surface that won't break off in the hand (coral *never* falls into this category). It is important that the diver has proper trim when using these techniques so that the feet do not drag and stir things up. This is another very relaxing and easy way to move around. When handholds are solid, this can be the strongest method of propulsion and is very useful in strong currents.

Webbed Gloves

Divers with good finger strength can add power to their arm stroke with the use of webbed gloves (see "Webbed Gloves"). The gloves' ef-

This diver has a good feet-up position as she pulls along the bottom but has forgotten to tuck in straps and hoses that may drag on the bottom, stirring things up.

fect is maximized by spreading and curving the fingers while stroking. These gloves make an impressive difference in strong currents, and when not in use, they should be kept in a BCD pocket.

Instrument Use

Divers who use the Gadget (see "The Gadget") have their instruments in front of their eyes at all times during a dive. Only if a diver surfaces to take compass bearings on landmarks above the water does the console require adjustment. Even then, the diver need only tilt the compass up to look through its side window.

To avoid damage from bumps and drops, the Gadget is usually assembled after the diver has entered the water and disassembled prior to doffing the equipment.

Most divers who do not use the Gadget pull a console up from their side when they need to monitor their gauges. Retrieving the console and studying the gauges generally requires enough time to interrupt the swim of divers who propel themselves with their arms. Pulling the console up and around can create enough drag to alter orientation in the water as well.

Divers may find that they can locate and read their gauges more quickly and with less disruption to their swim if they wear their gauges on their forearms either individually or on a console. A disadvantage of this method for divers who want to be able to gear up quickly and easily is that once the gauges are on the arms, they often snag on the BCD when the diver attempts to put it on. If the gauges are put on after the BCD, the diver is blocking the staging area that much longer while the gauges are strapped into place.

We know of no method for divers who swim with their arms to use a compass effectively underwater without the use of the Gadget.

Buddy Breathing

There are two methods by which buddies can share air when one has run out: (a) use of an octopus (a second regulator mouthpiece), and (b) the traditional method by which the buddies take turns breathing off the regulator connected to the tank with remaining air. The latter method requires the use of two hands. Consequently, a diver without an effective kick is unable to swim or maintain orientation while using this method properly. Use of this method, therefore, should *never* be included in the dive plan of any student or diver who uses the arms to swim. Only when both buddies are prepared to do an emergency out-of-air ascent when one of their air supplies is depleted should an arm-stroking diver dive without an octopus or dive with a buddy without an octopus.

Octopus Use

Divers who propel themselves with their arms normally place more distance between themselves and their buddies (to allow for the wide arc swing of their arms). This distance is greater than what is needed for a buddy to breathe from an octopus rigged on a standard length hose. To use a regular octopus, divers using an arm stroke to swim roll a bit on one side, facing the buddy, a bit above or below the buddy. While swimming on a slight angle, the arm swing is above the buddy and causes no problem. Buddy breathing is easier if the octopuses are rigged on a hose that is long enough to permit normal swimming. A longer hose gives all divers the advantage of more flexibility for maneuvering.

A breaststroking diver swims on her side to buddy-breathe off an octopus on a hose of regular length.

Experts hold different opinions regarding whether donors should give an out-of-air buddy their octopus or their primary regulator. One school of thought reasons that the panicky buddy, desperate for air, will attempt to seize the regulator in clear view, namely the one in the donor's mouth. Donors who are still in control and who know where they position their octopuses have a better opportunity to calmly find the alternate air source. The other school of thought reasons that if this exchange of regulators does not proceed smoothly and flawlessly, two divers will be without air. By retaining the primary regulator, donors increase the likelihood that at least one diver will remain in control and be able to help the out-of-air buddy. We strongly recommend that divers who swim and maintain orientation with their arms keep their primary regulators. Attaching the octopus to a readily accessible spot and frequently practicing freeing it and passing it to a buddy are essential.

Regulator Exchange Buddy Breathing

Divers without an octopus use the traditional buddy-breathing procedure in which they share air from one regulator. Although it is not recommended that divers who do it all with their arms ever plan

This octopus is readily visible to an out-of-air buddy and can also be located easily by the diver herself.

to use the regulator exchange buddy-breathing procedure for out-of-air emergencies, all divers should be trained in the technique and be indoctrinated to keep the skills current. In the event of an octopus failure, the need to share air with a nonbuddy diver in distress, or other unexpected contingency, the diver will be prepared to respond.

Regulator exchange requires both buddies to firmly grasp the mouthpiece or its hose with one hand and the buddy with the other hand. Holding the mouthpiece ensures that each buddy knows where it is and can get it back to the mouth even when it cannot be seen because visibility is bad. Holding the buddy ensures that the buddy who is out of air doesn't become separated from the air supply. Neither task can prudently be omitted. Nevertheless, divers who swim with their arms may need to release something momentarily in order to retain or regain body orientation and to begin a controlled ascent. In many cases, if one buddy kicks and can easily do so, that buddy should provide all the propulsion so both buddies can firmly grip each other and the regulator. In circumstances where this is not effective, divers who swim with their arms must swim with one hand and hold the regulator with the other hand. It is the regulator and not the buddy that should be firmly grasped, and when divers are the donees, they should remember that their grasp on the regulator is the only thing preventing them from losing all access to air.

Some instructors teach buddy breathing by having both students hold onto the donor's mouthpiece. Others prefer to have one or both of the students hold onto the hose rather than the mouthpiece. Students with limited manual dexterity should be encouraged to find the most effective method to grasp the regulator firmly.

The risks involved in one-handed buddy breathing make the use of an octopus an essential safety practice.

Gear Removal

Divers who do not walk up boat ladders or out of shallow water with many pounds of gear weighing them down remove their gear before leaving the water. The gear is passed to someone who can put it in a convenient location. Apparently because they can see it, helpers may ask for the tank first. The BCD naturally comes with it, leaving the weight belt and no positive buoyancy. This can present a problem for anyone and particularly for divers who do not have a strong kick that they can use to counterbalance the weight and keep their heads above water. The weight belt should always be handed out first or snapped on a line as described in the "Weight Belts" section. Because some people on the boat may ask for the BCD first, students should be so indoctrinated to remove the weight belt first that they do so as automatically as they blink.

If conditions permit, the diver should tuck regulators and the console inside the BCD before passing them out. This helps prevent the regulators and console from catching on a ladder step or being dragged through the mud. Helpers will most frequently be lifting the tank from an awkward position and may have difficulty protecting these items themselves.

When diving off a boat, it is a good idea to inform the captain and crew that you will remove your gear in the water and will need assistance bringing it back on board. Be sure to ask whoever helps pull the gear up to pile it all in an accessible place and not to disassemble it. Well-intended helpers have hoisted gear out of the water, taken it over mounds of clutter on deck, and deposited it where it was inaccessible to its owner and susceptible to damage.

Water Exits

Water exits are often difficult for divers who don't walk up ladders or slopes with their gear on. Whether assistance is needed and how it can best be provided is completely individualized. Each individual diver must usually work with each new situation before determining how best to cope with it.

Some students will be able to use their arms to hoist themselves out of a pool by pushing themselves up and onto the deck at a corner or side. Other students will need to be hoisted. This is easiest if two people standing on the pool deck each grab the student under one armpit for the lift. Students who are experienced swimmers will know which method is easiest for them to use in exiting a pool.

The easiest open-water exit is onto a water-level dive platform or step. For such an exit, the diver need only roll over onto the platform or step. Once secure on the platform or step, the diver can doff and pass up gear. Depending on what lies between the platform or step and the

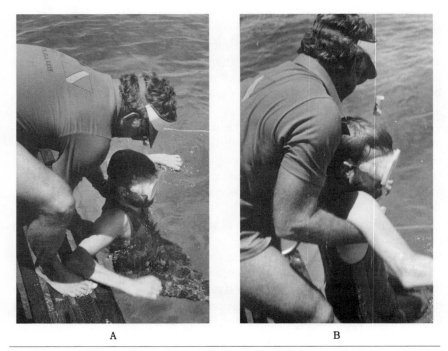

A   B

A buddy grabs a diver under the shoulders (photo A) and pulls him out of the water (photo B).

area the diver needs to approach, the diver may need assistance getting there. For example, if there are several steps or a ladder that must be negotiated, some divers may need help in the form of a steadying hand to enable them to walk up, others may need a shoulder or knee to push on to allow them to hoist themselves, and yet others might need two people to grab them under the armpits and hoist them up.

When there is no dive platform or water-level step, a diver's options are more limited. If there is a ladder, some divers will be able to use it and others will need to be hoisted from the water. Some divers will be able to use some ladders but not others, depending on how far into the water the steps extend, how they are spaced, how wide the ladder is, and how it connects with the boat or dock.

If the naturally occurring slope of the bottom leads up to land, most divers who do not walk will scoot along on their rumps until they reach their destination.

Some people are concerned about divers diving off a boat in moderately rough seas if they remove their gear in the water and need assistance entering the boat. This concern may stem from the fact that divers who walk up the ladder wearing their gear often forget that negotiating the ladder in rough seas requires more caution than negotiating a flight of steps on land. This lack of care often leads to injury. Divers who never walk up steps or ladders do not so inattentively approach the ladder. For these divers, steps are always a major obstacle necessitating considerable attention. Additionally, because the diver is removing gear in the water at the stern of the boat, the ladder is jerking around on the waves directly in front of the diver providing another reminder that caution is needed. Once attention is focused on avoiding harmful contact with the ladder, it is no great challenge to do so while removing gear and making an exit.

Diver Rescue

One of the first rescue techniques divers learn is how to tow another diver, whether conscious or unconscious, through the water. The usual way to do this, by using the arms to control the diver and the feet to provide propulsion, is not an option for divers who swim with their arms. These divers either must use one arm to control the diver and one to provide propulsion or find an armless way of controlling the diver so both hands can be used for propulsion.

A tired but conscious diver gets a tow by holding her buddy's foot. If she tucked the tower's knee between her body and her upper arm and held the foot in front of her, she would be more comfortable.

Fortunately, the most common situation in which towing may be needed involves a conscious but tired or distraught diver who needs only reassurance and some assistance. These divers are frequently able to help the rescuer. In this circumstance, rescuers who swim with their arms can simply instruct the victim to hold onto one of the rescuer's feet while the rescuer tows the victim and uses both hands for the swim stroke. It is easiest for victims, who will be lying on their backs during the tow, to tuck the leg between their arm and side and hold onto the foot. The rescuer, who will be swimming in the usual prone position, should maintain verbal contact with the victim as often as possible.

If a conscious victim is panicky and the rescuer wants to maintain closer visual and verbal contact with the victim, this towing technique is not possible. A cross-chest tow, allowing increased rescuer control, is needed. The rescuer swims on his or her strongest side alongside the victim, holding the victim with the other arm by the BCD or whatever permits a firm grasp across the victim's chest. The rescuer swims with the strong arm and pulls the victim along with the other.

Bringing an unconscious victim from the bottom to the surface is another important rescue technique. Each training agency teaches it differently, and any of their techniques can be used by divers who swim with their arms. One arm is used to control the victim while the other is used to control the ascent. Both the ascent itself and subsequent stability on the surface depend on the rescuers' buoyancy. Therefore, rescuers' primary concern should be their own buoyancy. If, when they reach the surface, the victim is too negatively buoyant, the rescuer can easily hold the victim on the surface long enough to add air to the victim's BCD. On the other hand, if rescuers are too negatively buoyant at the surface (having inflated the victim's BCD instead of their own), they may have a tendency unwittingly to push the victim underwater to support themselves or to lose control of the victim while they make their own adjustments.

Once an unconscious victim is on the surface, the rescuer begins artificial resuscitation (AR), and once a comfortable pattern of AR has been established, the rescuer also tows the victim toward the shore or boat. There are three common ways to do in-water AR: mouth-to-mouth, mouth-to-snorkle, and with the use of an AR mask. During mouth-to-mouth, the rescuer must hold the victim, pinch the victim's nose, tilt the victim's head back, turn the head toward the rescuer without submerging it, grab the victim for the tow, inflate the victim's lungs on the count of five, and tow the victim toward the boat or shore. This is a manageable, although unwieldy, number of tasks. If both the victim's and the rescuer's BCDs are properly inflated, the rescuer can hold the victim by gripping the chin at the jawbone in a manner that will both tilt the head back as needed and permit a tow. The other hand can be used to turn the victim's head and pinch the nose for the lung inflations and, between inflations, to provide propulsion for the tow with arm strokes. Although this is difficult and tiring for the rescuer, it may save the victim's life.

Mouth-to-snorkle should theoretically be easier than mouth-to-mouth because it is not necessary to turn the head and keep the mouth above water for the ventilations. Once the snorkle is in place and sealed, the rescuer moves behind the victim and begins the tow, either with both on their backs or with the victim on the back and the rescuer on a side. One hand is used to seal the snorkle, pinch the nose, and grasp under the chin to tilt the head back and facilitate the tow. The other hand is free for propulsion. (Some divers are taught to use the second hand to hold the bore end of the snorkle in place in their mouths or bent to keep out water. The effective use of teeth to hold the snorkle, lips to seal it for inflations, and tongue to keep water out of the snorkle

This rescuer gives mouth-to-snorkle artificial resuscitation while towing the victim back to the boat.

while letting the rescuer take in air makes this unnecessary.) Mouth-to-snorkle resuscitation is also slow and difficult but can be effective if mastered.

AR masks seal over a victim's nose and mouth and have a little port through which the rescuer can blow to inflate the victim's lungs. A short piece of surgical tubing can be attached to the port to allow the rescuer some distance from the victim's mouth. In-water scuba rescuers can use this combination to position themselves in a comfortable, efficient position for both AR and towing. The rescuer can choose whether to tow while swimming on a side or on the back. Because the tubing creates resistance and dead air space for carbon dioxide build-up, the smallest length of tubing that is effective should be used. As with the other techniques, the hand sealing the mask also grasps the victim under the chin for the tow, and the other hand is used for propulsion. Using an AR mask is probably the easiest and most flexible resuscitation method of the three. Its only disadvantage is that the diver must carry an extra piece of equipment on all dives. However, the mask is compact and fits easily in a BCD pocket, even with surgical tubing attached.

Rescuers using the towing techniques described in this chapter tow more slowly than comparably competent rescuers who propel the tow

A rescuer positions an artificial respiration mask on the victim's face before beginning a tow. The rescuer's hose is much too long, creating resistance and allowing unnecessary carbon dioxide buildup.

by kicking. If a rescuer with a strong kick *and* rescue training and ability is available, the tow should be transferred to that diver as soon as possible. But if such a rescuer is not immediately available, a slow tow is better than no tow.

Use of Lights

When divers wear their lights attached to their bodies or gear, they must make a special effort not to shine the light inadvertently in the eyes of nearby divers. This is especially important when divers wear a light on their heads. When they look at their buddies, the light will likely be shining directly in their buddy's eyes. To avoid this, the diver can simply tilt the head up and look at other divers as though through the bottom of bifocals.

Divers with lights attached to their heads will have to give signals either by moving their entire heads or by reaching up to manipulate the light manually. If lights are mounted elsewhere, such as on a belt, manual manipulation will be required. At least one light should be worn in a manner that allows it enough movement to make signalling possible.

Line Use

There are several methods that divers who swim with their arms can use to follow a line. The circumstances of the dive will dictate which method is appropriate. Where visibility is clear and a sudden and complete loss of visibility is unlikely, divers can simply swim alongside the line. If they also swim a little above and over it, they can stay close enough to it to grab it quickly without the sweep of their arm stroke disturbing the line. When visibility is not clear but no less than 2 feet, the diver can swim along the line so that it is always in the bend of the elbow and touching the inside of the arm. The line is in sight as well as within reach, and even through a wet suit, the line can be felt without putting undue pressure on it.

When visibility is less than 2 feet, the diver should maintain constant contact with the line. Divers who swim with their arms can modify

A diver follows a line, keeping the line in the bend of her elbow.

A diver can also follow a line by keeping the line in the V formed by the thumb and forefinger as the diver breaststrokes.

the traditional method of keeping the line inside the "O" formed by their thumb and forefinger making the "OK" signal. The line is kept against the "V" formed by the thumb and index finger, but the fingers are spread as they are when doing a regular breaststroke for needed propulsion. The stroke may need to be shortened for the hand to maintain contact with the line. Speed is only slightly reduced by this modification of the stroke. If there is any doubt that this method will be completely reliable in the particular circumstances of a dive, a one-handed dog paddle stroke (see "Propulsion") should be used instead. It provides less speed but permits holding the line with the closed "OK" hand shape.

Usually when divers are following lines, they need to be oriented in a slight feet-up position to avoid kicking up silt on the bottom. Divers whose feet don't move themselves find that this position also helps avoid tangling the feet in the line as they follow it through twists and turns. Divers who lack feeling in their legs and feet should consciously make it a point to check for possible entanglements of their legs and feet whenever they cross lines, change the side of the line they are swimming along, change direction on the line, or follow a twist or turn. They may also want to consider avoiding being the last person on the line. A buddy behind them could quickly discover and correct an accidental entanglement.

Divers who swim with their arms can most easily lay a line by using a line reel with a long handle and a breaking device (see "Line Reels"). Once the line is attached at its first point, the line reel can be tucked into a belt. With the breaking device adjusted to keep a steady but moderate tension in the line, the diver can swim with the line unwinding automatically. Whenever necessary, the diver can pull the line reel out of the belt to tie off. The diver should tuck the line reel carefully into the belt and maintain a focus on it to make sure that it does not become dislodged and fall away unnoticed.

Instead of securing the line reel to the diver by tucking a long handle into a belt, the diver may attach it with a snap hook. Although this makes securing and releasing the line reel a two-handed, more time-consuming task, it also makes dropping and losing the reel virtually impossible.

Reeling in the line is more of a challenge. Unless the diver finds or invents a self-retracting line reel, two hands are needed to reel in the line. For divers whose propulsion comes from their arms, this means that no propulsion is possible while reeling in the line because these divers will be pulling themselves along the line as they reel it in. This fact should be considered both when selecting a line to use and when tying off. Strong line and secure tie-offs are crucial. Holding the reel with one hand and turning the crank with the other, divers reel in the line and themselves and must keep the line taut at the same time. The diver can free one hand momentarily (for adjusting buoyancy or adding propulsion) by holding the crank still with the same hand that holds the reel. Extra care must be taken to keep the line taut during this process.

Reeling in a line is unusually difficult and important in the circumstances that necessitate the use of a line. The lives of every member of the dive team depend on the line being reeled in without breaking or becoming loose and entangled. Divers who don't kick should practice this technique extensively if they will be diving where lines are needed, but they should plan to use the technique only as an emergency measure if another diver who kicks becomes unable to reel in the line.

Lift Bag Use

Divers who use their arms for propulsion can make easier use of a lift bag with a deflate valve and cord than one without. Instead of struggling to tilt the bag only enough to let the proper amount of air escape, the diver merely pulls the deflate cord. If two hands are required, it is only momentarily.

Divers should avoid the temptation to free their hands by clipping the lift bag to themselves while working at depth or during an ascent. A diver focused on the task at hand may not notice changes in depth that are significant enough to expand the air in the lift bag, dragging an attached diver into an ascent. During the ascent, air in the bag will expand, causing it to rise more and more quickly unless the air is dumped. The possibility of the diver losing control of the lift bag and being dragged along for an out-of-control ascent is too great when the lift bag is clipped to the diver.

Matters for the Classroom

4

Matters for the Classroom

4

The Tables and the Bends

Sport divers use the U.S. Navy Dive Tables to avoid decompression sickness, popularly known as the bends. The Tables help divers prevent the cause of the bends, the release of a dangerous amount of nitrogen bubbles into their blood and tissues as they reduce the pressure exerted on their bodies when they ascend to the surface. Even in a basic class, instructors do more than explain how to use the Tables to create a safe dive plan. Understanding why the Tables work is important to safety, so instructors also describe how the Tables were developed and how their derivation affects their use by sport divers.

One of the techniques the Navy used in developing the Tables was tissue averaging. The body is composed of different types of tissues (fat, muscle, etc.), and each type of tissue absorbs and releases nitrogen at different rates and in different quantities. Rather than trying to develop a maze of tables to account for each combination of tissues in each individual, tissue averaging assumes that the combination of tissues in every human body is the same and that each tissue absorbs and releases nitrogen at the same average rate. The average tissue profile used was that of the average Navy diver. It was for this average Navy diver that the Tables were intended to be effective. Any variation from this average diver (in age, weight, build, physical condition, sex, and so forth) will affect the application of the Tables to any particular sport diver.

Some specialists in underwater medicine believe that unused tissues, like those in a paralyzed limb, may release gas at a different rate than the hypothetical average tissue. Additionally, safe nitrogen uptake and elimination are dependent on blood circulation. Divers with little or no effective use of one or more limbs have reduced blood circulation. These factors have caused different authorities to make different recommendations regarding use of the Tables. Some have said that people with disabilities should not dive because they are more prone to the bends. Others advocate limiting diving to depths of 27 feet or less, where it is theoretically impossible to get the bends. Still others say there is no need to establish any different decompression rules for disabled divers than for other divers.

There have been no studies that can be used to establish a scientific base for Table modifications that take various disabilities into account. Lacking scientific data, divers are looking to the experience of other divers with similar disabilities and are using this empirical data to guide their own dive planning. Although droves of disabled divers have been diving with the Tables, we are aware of no reported instance of the bends among them. Many divers interpret this as an indication that their prudent use of the Tables enables them to dive safely.

All divers are advised to add an extra margin of safety in their use of the Tables, in recognition of their differences from the hypothetical average Navy diver. These extra safety measures are necessary, for example, if the diver is overweight, old, female, physically underfit, or a smoker. Many divers analogize disabilities that affect circulation and possibly the rate at which tissues gas off to these factors that require the use of a safety margin.

Although responsible divers often add a safety margin to protect them in their use of the Tables, there is no set formula for doing so. Each diver assesses his or her differences and decides how cautious to be. Many divers have adapted a rule used by Navy divemasters for adjusting the Tables for dives under arduous or cold conditions. This rule requires the diver to assume a bottom time 10 minutes longer than the actual bottom time. Some divers extend the rule for extra safety by adding both 10 minutes of bottom time and 10 feet of depth. Other divers use a rule requiring them to stay well under the single dive limits on the first dive, then, when they determine their repetitive group designation for a second dive, they automatically increase their designation by one or two letter groups.

By whatever method, all divers are responsible for safe application of the Navy Dive Tables to their own circumstances, given the conditions of each individual dive. Empirical data suggest that disabled divers are at least as successful in fulfilling this responsibility as are overweight, out-of-shape, smoking, older, or female divers.

Thermoregulation

Water conducts heat away from the body, chilling it so much more rapidly than air does that basic scuba courses include a discussion of hypothermia. Students are taught that water temperatures that seem warm to those who normally think in terms of air temperatures are in fact cold enough that divers must be constantly alert to the danger of hypothermia in themselves and other members of their dive party. Students are also taught that shivering is the first sign of hypothermia and that they should end a dive if shivering begins. These warnings should be communicated particularly strongly and effectively to students with extensive paralysis. These students know that their decreased circulation causes them to chill more quickly than other people with similar builds. Although they can feel themselves growing cold (even though they may lack sensation in parts of their bodies), they are at least as likely as other students to underestimate the seriousness of becoming chilled. If they submit to the temptation to continue a dive and then sit wet and cold during a long boat ride or surface interval, hypothermia may result.

During in-class orientation to checkout dives, instructors often describe the environment in which students will be diving. Instructors should take this opportunity to inform students of the weather conditions they are likely to encounter as well. Almost all dives involve exposure to extremes of temperature, not only in the water but also en route. If students prone to chilling know ahead of time that there will be a long, wet, windy boat ride back to land, for example, they can prepare for it by bringing along warm, dry, water-repellent clothes.

Warm temperatures are equally troublesome for individuals who don't sweat, such as many people with spinal cord injuries. Without sweating, the body has no natural way to cool itself, so hyperthermia is a potential problem. Pouring water on the skin acts like an artificial sweat and cools the body effectively. If a long boat ride will make it uncomfortable or inconvenient for students to be doused with water, they can bring along a mister with fresh water.

Students who overheat or chill easily may want to pack a mister or a pocket-sized, reflective emergency blanket for a dive trip.

Currents

No matter where a basic course is given and what the local diving conditions are, instructors warn students of the dangers of currents. The warning is often a simple reminder to students to assess the current before leaping into it and to avoid swimming against currents that are too difficult. Students are told that a 1-knot (1.13 mph) current is commonly considered the strongest current against which a diver can make headway.

Divers who use arm strokes often wonder how this applies to them and how they will fare in a strong current. As with any diver, disabled divers' abilities to handle the current will depend upon their strength, conditioning, planning, and coolheadedness. Whenever current is a factor, a diver with less strength has less margin for error than a stronger diver when other characteristics, such as fitness and confidence, are equal. Divers with less strength, therefore, must dive that much smarter. A knowledge of where and when to expect currents is necessary to safe dive planning. A training dive in water with a mild current would also be invaluable.

A current is the horizontal movement of water. Currents exist in almost any body of water and may be generated by any number of factors, including movement of the earth, river outflows, underwater springs, waterfalls, tides, wind, shore topography, and so forth. The currents that divers are most likely to encounter are (a) wind currents, (b) tidal and longshore currents, and (c) subsurface ocean currents.

Wind Currents

Wind currents are caused by the force of the wind blowing across the water, moving the surface layer of water. They are significant for sport divers because, among other reasons, they create surface currents. Depending on their strength, surface currents can be hazardous for the diver. Surface currents are usually most pronounced in the open ocean or on large inland bodies of water, where the large expanse of water permits the effect of the wind to gain force.

A surface current may not run in the same direction that the wind blows. Because of the effects of the earth's rotation, the direction of the current will vary from about 15 degrees to the right in shallow coastal waters to about 45 degrees to the right in deep ocean areas (south of the equator, it will vary from 15 to 45 degrees to the left). The speed of the current depends on the wind's speed, consistency, and duration, and other factors. In general, a surface current is about 2% as strong as the wind (thus a 15-knot wind can generate a wind current of about one third of a knot).

The best technique for dealing with wind currents is to dive below the surface as soon as possible. When diving from the shore, a diver can do this once in deep enough water. When diving from a boat, the diver will usually have to fight the wind current long enough to move from the stern to the anchor line before beginning the descent. When any surface current is present during an entry and descent, use of a current line, rigged from the entry point at the stern to the anchor line, is an essential safety procedure. Divers pull themselves against the current along the line. When divers have finished their ascent, at the end of the dive, surface current is again a factor. To avoid being carried downwind by a current that may have picked up while they were underwater, divers should be sure to ascend with a firm grasp on the anchor line and to move to the stern holding the current line. A long (150-foot) trailing line that floats freely behind the boat allows divers who missed the anchor line or released the current line another chance to grab hold. It also provides divers with a safe way to wait their turn to reboard without having to fight the current.

Current lines are generally unnecessary on walk-on dive boats in the luxury dive spots like the Florida Keys. Because these boats usually operate in calm weather and serve novice divers, they generally don't go out under the conditions that necessitate current lines. Nevertheless, before entering the water, divers should assess the current by watching how quickly the buoy at the end of the trailing line moves away from the boat. When divers fall off the back of these boats, they should assess the current again by noting whether they are drifting away from the boat. If there is any suggestion of a current, divers should

A diver moves from the stern to the anchor line following a current line.

descend quickly and, at the end of the dive, resurface directly upcurrent of the boat.

Tidal and Longshore Currents

Tidal currents are the water's horizontal movements generated by the rise and fall of the tide. The tide rises until it reaches a maximum height, called high tide or high water, and then falls to a minimum level, called low tide or low water. This cycle generally occurs twice in each lunar day, which averages 24 hours and 50 minutes. The rate of rise and fall is not uniform. From low water, the tide rises slowly at first but at an increasing rate until it is about halfway between high and low water. At the halfway point, its rate of rise begins to decrease until it has reached high water, when the rise ceases. Between high and low water, a similar change in the rate of fall occurs. The tidal currents correspond to the tidal rise and fall and are most pronounced in the beach and near offshore shallow waters. During the rise of the tide, the current comes in and is called a flood current or flood tide, and during its fall, the associated current goes out and is called an ebb current or ebb tide. The velocity of these currents varies.

Divers should plan their beach dives to avoid being swept out to sea and, in fact, can put the current to good use. At the exact high and low tide, there is no appreciable tidal current. During a flood tide, the current pushes the diver toward shore, and during an ebb tide, it pulls the diver away from shore. For the sport diver, then, the ideal time to begin a beach dive is about a half hour before the low tide, when the diver benefits from a very slight ebbing of the tide to help reach deep water, from slack water for the dive, and from a slight flood current to assist in returning to the beach. At no time should a diver begin a beach or near-shore dive more than about a half hour into an ebb tide.

Although tidal currents usually create water movement directly toward or away from the shore, they can change into longshore currents, which run parallel to shore, due to topographical features such as jetties, piers, marinas, reef, sandbars, coves, and so forth. Longshore currents can also be generated by the large movements of water associated with nearby river outflows and waterfalls and by waves against the shoreline. The direction of a longshore current can vary greatly in a small area. In a small cove, for example, the U shape of the cove can cause longshore currents in opposite directions on each side of the U. Longshore currents are important to the diver because they make it difficult to swim directly back to the entry point. When returning at the end of the dive, divers will have to offset their course to compensate for the effects of the longshore current.

Subsurface Ocean Currents

Subsurface currents exist only at depths beneath the surface. They may be nearly constant currents such as the equatorial currents generated largely by the trade winds, or they may be more temporary currents generated by conditions such as storms. The seasonal meandering of the major ocean currents such as the Gulf Stream or California Current, coupled with underwater topography, weather, earthquakes, and so forth, change the direction and location of subsurface currents throughout the year.

Subsurface currents are most frequently encountered during wreck diving and wall diving. Divers must recognize their presence and quickly assess the wisdom of diving in the current conditions found on each dive. As always, diver judgment and discretion are the key to safe diving. If the diver reaches a wreck and discovers the subsurface current is too strong for safe diving within physical and equipment limitations, the diver should cancel the dive and ascend the anchor line to the boat. Similarly, when a current is encountered during a wall dive, the prudent diver should ascend to a shallower portion of the reef beyond the effect of the current. A diver should never hesitate to cancel a dive when the current is too strong.

Conclusion

Under controlled situations, diving in a current can be enjoyable and safe. Drift dives are available in some locations. On a drift dive, divers simply let the current carry them over the reef while the dive boat follows on the surface to recover divers down-current at the end of the dive. Drift diving is among the easiest, most pleasant diving and shouldn't be missed.

The sea, and indeed almost any aquatic environment, can overpower any diver. The lack of a strong kick is a disadvantage in these situations. However, many disabled divers, accustomed to dealing on a daily basis with a hostile environment, have developed a look-before-you-leap attitude and an ability to plan and cope that are advantageous in trying circumstances and that may compensate for any lack of physical strength. Disabled divers need not feel more intimidated than others by the prospect of challenging diving.

Appendix   **A**

Introduction to Selected Disabilities

The words commonly used to describe disabilities are rather imprecise. One set of words describes the disability in terms of loss of limb or function, such as paraplegia, quadriplegia, or amputation. Another set identifies the source of the disability, such as polio, cerebral palsy, or spinal cord injury. Often the two sets are joined, as in post-polio paraplegic or spinal cord-injured quadriplegic. Because the first set of terms describes conditions extremely diverse and the second set describes illnesses or injuries that affect each person differently, the classifications, even when used jointly, are not as helpful as their popularity may imply. This is why we have avoided using them and have identified instead the exact functional limitation that pertained to a particular discussion. Nevertheless, these words describe a broad range of characteristics and are commonly used for that reason. The following descriptions reflect how the words are commonly used in the disability community. They may bear little relation to technical, medical definitions.

Categories of Functional Limitations

Paraplegia refers to a partial or complete loss of function from the waist down. If the functional loss has been partial, a person with paraplegia, often labeled paraplegic, may walk with the assistance of braces, crutches, or canes or, like those with a more complete loss of function, may use a wheelchair. Paraplegics often develop increased upper body strength.

Quadriplegia refers to a loss of function from the neck or chest down. Although there is a reduced manual dexterity, some degree of shoulder and arm strength may be retained. Someone labeled quadriplegic may be totally unable to move anything below the neck or chest or might, in rare instances, be able to walk despite some loss of function throughout the body. Most fall somewhere between the totally paralyzed and the "walking quad." Most quadriplegics use either a manual or an electric wheelchair. Walking quads often use one or two canes. Quadriplegia may involve a reduction in respiratory strength. Some quads may have no difficulty breathing, whereas others may have to put some effort into it.

Amputation refers to a loss of limb. Amputees may have lost one or both arms and/or one or both legs. There are all manner of labels for amputees that generally describe their loss. For example, a bilateral above-the-knee amputee refers to a person who lost each leg from a point somewhere above the knee. A single below-the-elbow amputee refers to a person who lost one arm from somewhere below the elbow. The amount of limb left intact, called the stump, is not specified. Thus, an above-the-knee amputee might have enough stump left to provide good balance and stability and to use an artificial limb or might have no stump at all. Some amputees use artificial limbs, or prosthetics; others do not. Some leg amputees use walking aids like crutches or canes, some use wheelchairs, and others walk with no difficulty.

Spasticity involves spasms or tightening of the muscles that may range from rare to occasional to frequent to constant. "Spastic" is not an acceptable label to describe people with spasticity, and in fact no such label exists.

Sources of Disability

Polio, not currently the threat it was during the epidemics of the 1950s and earlier, has left a number of people with a variety of disabilities. In a generally hit-and-miss fashion, polio destroys the nerves that send messages to the muscles. It can affect some or all of the muscles in some or all parts of the body. The affected muscles may be completely or partially weakened. Thus, a polio survivor (the term currently in vogue) may have no functional limitations, a mild arm weakness, or quadriplegia or paraplegia (or possibly hemoplegia, in which the loss of function runs the length of one side of the body). One form of polio also affects respiration, again in its unpredictable mild-to-severe manner. Polio generally does not affect bowel and bladder control or sensation, but affected areas seem to be significantly more susceptible to chilling.

Spinal cord injury is a frequent cause of disability. Vehicular accidents, sports accidents, and war account for the bulk of spinal cord injuries. The spinal cord can be injured anywhere along its length. Parts of the body at or below the level of the injury are affected. The higher the injury, the more of the body that is affected. People with spinal cord injuries sometimes use the location of their injury as a shorthand description of their disability. Thus a C-3 quad is one whose cord was damaged at the level of the third cervical vertebra and who is affected from that level of the neck down, whereas a T-2 para was injured at the second thoracic vertebra and is affected only from the midtorso down. The cord can be either completely or partially severed or damaged. The former accounts for completely paralyzed quads and the latter for walking quads. Differences in the extent of the damage to the cord also account for differences in the amount and nature of sensation remaining in the affected areas. All sensation is lost with a completely severed cord, but sensation may be only partially lost or distorted if the cord is partially damaged. Spinal cord injury usually involves a loss of bladder and bowel control, which is compensated for by the use of urine-collection bags or intermittent self-catheterization and a fairly rigid bowel program. Loss of the ability to sweat and some degree of spasticity are other common results of spinal cord injury.

Cerebral palsy (CP) usually results from a birth injury to the brain but is sometimes acquired in early childhood following a head injury. CP can cause any degree of spasticity, uncontrolled muscle movements, poor balance and coordination, and difficulty walking and articulating speech. The speech impediments of people with CP are often mistaken as indicators of retardation. Although retardation is possible in people with CP, as it is in others, its presence is not indicated by difficulty speaking. People with CP may walk with or without difficulty or may use a manual wheelchair; an electric wheelchair; a taller, narrower, motorized three-wheeled vehicle; or a combination of these. Some talk without difficulty and others use a speech board on which they point to words or letters to communicate. Most fall in between.

Spina bifida is a condition caused by an opening in an infant's back that exposes or through which may protrude portions of the spinal cord. Modern surgical procedures close the lesion and may reduce the damage caused to the spinal cord. To the extent the damage goes un-corrected, spina bifida is a form of spinal cord injury and may cause paralysis, loss of sensation, and loss of bladder and bowel control. Like others with spinal cord injuries, people with spina bifida may appear unaffected, may use electric wheelchairs, or anything in between.

Multiple sclerosis (MS) is a chronic disease that may lead to paraly-sis, visual impairment, loss of balance, shaking of limbs, speech defects, fatigue, and loss of bladder and bowel control. It is caused by the hardening of patches of tissue in the brain and spinal cord. These patches block the messages being sent along the nerves. The effects of MS vary depending on the location of the hardened tissues, and con-sequently its effects vary greatly from individual to individual. For unknown reasons, the progress of the disease occasionally stops and stabilizes for some time. At other times, often in conjunction with un-related stresses, deterioration accelerates. MS is now being treated ex-perimentally, and apparently successfully, with hyperbaric oxygen.

Appendix   **B**

Forms for Self-Identification and Access Evaluation

These forms are intended to collect information that will make it easier for disabled divers or would-be divers to find each other, to find experienced instructors, and to learn about the accessibility of dive shops and sites.

Please make several copies of each form so you can send additional information as you acquire it. Print or type the information requested and send it to Leisure Press, Box 5076, Champaign, IL 61820, marked to the attention of "Dive Manual."

Form 1: Disabled Divers

This form collects identifying information from and about disabled divers so that other interested persons can contact them. If you know of any disabled divers, please give them a copy of this form. Although we want to collect as much information as possible, we don't want to invade anyone's privacy by listing them without their consent. If a diver feels uncomfortable providing any of the information requested, that information can simply be omitted.

Form 2: Instructors of Disabled Divers

This form collects identifying information from and about instructors who have had experience teaching students with disabilities. Please pass it along to anyone you know who should be listed.

Forms 3 and 4: Accessibility of Shops, Boats, and Sites

These two forms are both intended to collect access information from disabled divers or students about the shops, boats, and dive sites they have visited. As the information is amassed, it will become a central access guide to diving and will help divers find convenient diving.

Both forms list various facilities and pathways in or around shops and boats (Form 3) and dive sites not reached by boat (Form 4). Please make notes about each of these aspects of accessibility. If a shop or site is associated with a hotel, restaurant, or other facility, as is common at Caribbean resorts, please note the accessibility of those associated facilities in the "comments" section.

Form 1:   Disabled Divers

Name: _____

Address: _____

_____

_____

Home phone: _____

Work phone: _____

Type of disability: _____

Began diving: 19 _____

Certifications:

Course	*Agency*	*Year*
_____	_____	_____
_____	_____	_____
_____	_____	_____
_____	_____	_____
_____	_____	_____
_____	_____	_____
_____	_____	_____

_____ (number) dives logged as of _____ (date)

Form 2: *Instructors of Disabled Divers*

Name: _____

Address: _____

_____

_____

Home phone: _____

Work phone: _____

Shop phone: _____

Experience with what disabilities: _____

_____

_____

Began diving: 19_____   Began teaching: 19_____

Instructor Certifications:

Title	Agency	Year
_____	_____	_____
_____	_____	_____
_____	_____	_____
_____	_____	_____
_____	_____	_____

Form 3: Accessibility of Shops and Boats

Name: _____

Address: _____

_____

Phone: _____

Parking: _____

_____

Parking to shop entrance: _____

_____

Entrance: _____

_____

Interior: _____

_____

Equipment area: _____

_____

Bathrooms: _____

_____

Shower: _____

_____

Shop to dock: _____

_____

Parking to dock: _____

_____

Dock to first boat (specify name): _____

_____

Boat interior: _____

_____

Boat into water: _____

_____

Water to boat: _____

_____

Dock to 2nd boat (name): _____

_____

Boat interior: _____

_____

Boat into water: _____

_____

Water to boat: _____

_____

Other comments: _____

_____

Information submitted by:

Name: _____

Address: _____

             _____

Phone: _____

Form 4: Accessibility of Sites

Site name: _____

Address: _____

_____

_____

Phone: _____

Parking: _____

_____

Parking to entry: _____

_____

Entry point: _____

_____

Into water: _____

_____

Route to bathrooms: _____

_____

Bathrooms: _____

_____

Route to showers: _____

_____

Showers: _____

_____

_____

Route to picnic areas: _____

_____

Picnic areas: _____

_____

Route to vending: _____

_____

Vending areas: _____

_____

Route to camping: _____

_____

Camping areas: _____

_____

Other comments: _____

_____

_____

_____

_____

Information submitted by:

Name: _____

Address: _____

              _____

              _____

Phone: _____

Appendix   **C**

Organizations and Other Resources

From "Selecting an Instructor and Club" (Part 1)

National Association of Scuba Diving Schools
641 West Willow St.
Long Beach, CA 90806

National Association of Underwater Instructors
P.O. Box 14650
4650 Arrow Highway, Suite F-1
Montclair, CA 91763

National YMCA Underwater Activities
Oakbrook Square
6083-A Oakbrook Pkwy.
Norcross, GA 30092

Professional Association of Diving Instructors
1243 East Warner Ave.
Santa Ana, CA 92705

Scuba Schools International
1449 Riverside Dr.
Ft. Collins, CO 80524

Students generally deal with a local instructor certified by one of these agencies, rather than with the agency itself.

From "Webbed Gloves" (Part 2)

The webbed gloves referred to in Part 2, "Webbed Gloves" are available by mail order from Eddie Bauer and from The Finals. Eddie Bauer's glove is called a "powerstroke swimglove," item #A117E, and it may be ordered from the company at Fifth & Union, P.O. Box 3700, Seattle, WA 98130-0006 (800-426-8020). The Finals' glove is called a "swimit," item #490, and it may be ordered from them at 21 Minisink Ave., Port Jervis, NY 12771 (800-452-0452). Another mail-order firm, Early Winters, also once sold the "powerstroke swimglove." Early Winters has gone out of business but is expected to reopen in Chicago.

From "Fins" (Part 2)

National Handicapped Sports and Recreation Association
425 13th St., NW
Washington, DC 20004

From "Regulators and Octopuses" (Part 2)

Undercurrents is available from Undercurrents, P.O. Box 1658, Sausalito, CA 94965.

All of the diving equipment mentioned throughout the book is available (if at all) at or through local professional dive shops.

About the Authors

Jill Robinson is a disabled diver who had polio in 1955 and gets around on land in a wheelchair. She began diving in 1982 and logs 60 to 70 dives a season. Jill holds specialty certifications in night diving, deep diving, wreck diving, search and recovery diving, Scuba Lifesaving and Accident Management, and cavern and cave diving, and she has completed assistant instructor training. She has been a teaching assistant in classes with both able-bodied and disabled students and has dived with a number of disabled divers from around the country. Jill has been involved in efforts to open sport diving to people with a variety of disabilities since the first national meeting of disabled divers, instructors, training agency representatives, and other interested parties.

An attorney specializing in disability rights and personal injury matters, Jill counts among her publications the most effective regulation prohibiting discrimination on the basis of handicap promulgated by any federal agency. As a plaintiff's personal injury attorney, she had a major role in preparing for trial a case which resulted in a $5 million jury verdict. Jill now runs a consulting business that assists personal injury attorneys in assessing and demonstrating the impact of their clients' injuries.

A. Dale Fox taught Jill much of what she knows about diving. Dale has been diving since 1971 and teaching diving since 1976. He is a PADI master instructor, a NAUI instructor, and an instructor for the National Speleological Society. He has certified more than 600 divers and has taught a number of disabled divers. As an active Red Cross water safety, first-aid, and CPR instructor, Dale is able to teach his students the range of skills and knowledge they need to become safe and responsible divers.

Recently retired from the Navy, Dale was a commissioned officer serving as the personal aide and flag secretary to the Commander of the Military Sealift Command. Prior to that assignment, he served as a U.S. Navy commissioned officer and as a member of the U.S. delegation to the SALT II negotiations.

Dale is now managing a dive shop in northern Virginia.

Notes